Tim Chester has done the church in the U[...]
ful analysis at its best, supplemented by sc[...]
and ideas for reaching a part of British c[...]
represented in the life of the national chu[...]
that the under-represented are not the unreached!

Stephen Gaukroger, Director of Clarion Trust International and former President of the Baptist Union

This book is the fruit of passionate engagement of local churches with struggling neighbourhoods across the UK. It offers flashes of penetrating insight and perception into the challenges and opportunities of ministry in our more deprived areas.

Frog Orr-Ewing, Rector of Latimer Minster and Chaplain and Missioner to the Oxford Centre for Christian Apologetics

This is excellent; it breaks new ground, is outspoken and provocative, but issues a straightforward challenge which the evangelical community in the UK desperately needs to hear. In some places it will not be popular, but it is absolutely clear that the writing is driven by a missionary passion and by a profound desire to see truth transforming areas of our society which for far too long have been closed off to effective Christian witness because of the middle-class captivity of the majority of congregations. The work is enhanced by being based on actual experience, both of Tim and the colleagues he draws into this narrative, and it is further enriched by the intensely practical nature of its conclusions and suggestions.

David Smith, Senior Research Fellow at International Christian College, Glasgow, and author of a number of books on Christian mission, including Seeking a City with Foundations *(IVP)*

Tim Chester has worked hard to show how the raw, uncut gospel must be applied in the 'unreached' people groups of once 'Christian' nations. He writes from both ministry experience and a passion for the gospel. He is also wised-up about the missional challenges before us, bringing valuable practical insight and needed advice for the reader.

Joel Virgo, Church Elder, Church of Christ the King, Brighton

UNREACHED

UNREACHED

GROWING CHURCHES in WORKING-CLASS and DEPRIVED AREAS

TIM CHESTER

ivp

INTER-VARSITY PRESS
Norton Street, Nottingham NG7 3HR, England
Email: ivp@ivpbooks.com
Website: www.ivpbooks.com

First published 2012

British Library Cataloguing in Publication Data
A catalogue record for this book is available from the British Library.

ISBN: 978-1-84474-603-3

Set in Garamond 12/15pt
Typeset in Great Britain by CRB Associates, Potterhanworth, Lincolnshire
Printed in Great Britain by Ashford Colour Press Ltd, Gosport, Hampshire

*Inter-Varsity Press publishes Christian books that are true to the Bible and that communicate
the gospel, develop discipleship and strengthen the church for its mission in the world.*

*Inter-Varsity Press is closely linked with the Universities and Colleges Christian Fellowship,
a student movement connecting Christian Unions in universities and colleges throughout Great
Britain, and a member movement of the International Fellowship of Evangelical Students.
Website: www.uccf.org.uk*

CONTENTS

INTRODUCTION

Think of the thriving evangelical churches in your area, and the chances are they will be in the 'nice' areas of town and their leaders will be middle class.

I once attended a lecture at which the speaker showed a map of my city, Sheffield. The council wards were coloured different shades, according to a series of social indicators: educational achievement, household income, benefit recipients, social housing, criminal activity, and so on. Slide after slide showed that the east side of the city was the needy, socially deprived half, compared to the more prosperous west. Where are the churches? Counting all the various tribes of evangelicalism, the large churches are on the west side. The working-class and deprived areas of our cities are not being reached with the gospel. There are many exciting exceptions, but the pattern is clear. According to Mez McConnell from Niddrie Community Church in Edinburgh, of the fifty worst housing schemes in Scotland, half have no church, and most of the others only have a dying church. Very few have an evangelical witness. This book is about reaching those unreached areas.

Research conducted for Tearfund in 2007 shows that churchgoing in the UK is a middle-class pursuit.[1] Adults in social grades AB (professionals, senior and middle management) are over-represented among both regular and occasional churchgoers. Meanwhile, adults of social grade C2 and D (skilled, semi-skilled and unskilled manual) have the highest proportion of non-churched. Julian Rebera from New Life Church in Brighton concludes, 'There are very few churches on deprived estates. Those that exist are not attended by people from the estates, but by people outside the estates. And very few people from the estates travel out to our city-centre, largely white, middle-class churches.'

Yet it was not always like this. The Great Awakening was largely a working-class movement. Although its leaders were middle class, the Establishment treated their open-air preaching with scorn. Instead, it was working-class people who flocked to hear John Wesley and George Whitefield. Wesley organized converts into 'classes' and 'societies'. These were lay-led, often by working-class or lower-middle-class individuals. Robert Wearmouth says,

> Methodism gained its greatest successes among the socially distressed and ostracised among the labouring masses. Never claiming to be a class or partisan movement, always emphasising the universal love of God, its most urgent appeals were addressed to the common people . . . The higher classes in English society were scarcely touched by Methodist influence, but the working men and women were profoundly affected.[2]

The Industrial Revolution saw increased social stratification. It was during this time that middle-class and working-class identities began to emerge. And in the late eighteenth and early nineteenth centuries, evangelicalism appealed disproportionately to skilled artisans, according to historian David Bebbington.[3] Skilled artisans made up 23% of the population, but 59% of evangelical Nonconformists fell into this category. Both unskilled labourers and the middle classes were underrepresented in Nonconformist ranks. Methodists made a greater impact on labourers, but the proportion of Methodists who were labourers (16%) was still just below the proportion in society as a whole (17%). By the mid-1800s, perhaps half the UK population attended church. But contemporaries remarked that the labouring population was largely absent. Many congregations in mining areas were predominantly working class, but the majority of the working classes were not worshippers. In the late nineteenth century, the trend towards class-specific suburbs accelerated, and church attendance varied accordingly. Middle-class Ealing had 47% attendance, while working-class Fulham had 12%. Religious practice was becoming more directly associated with class. This was accentuated by the upward mobility of churchgoers. By the 1930s, almost half of Methodist members were in non-manual occupations, and by the 1970s it was three-quarters.

So why have we evangelicals been so ineffectual at reaching the urban poor, despite our origins? Here are a number of possible reasons.[4]

1. The parochial system of the Church of England was ill-equipped to cope with the rapid urbanization of the Industrial Revolution. Meanwhile, independent churches had no system for reallocating funds to the new urban centres, into which the population was moving. Today there are some good responses to this mismatch of resources. Christ Church, the

large evangelical Anglican church in the prosperous Sheffield suburb of Fulwood, provides generous support to churches in poorer parishes in the region. Nevertheless, typically, urban churches are under-resourced.

2. Churchgoing has been perceived, both by non-churchgoers and many churchgoers, to be a respectable activity demanding 'Sunday-best' clothes and clean living. So the poor have often felt unable to attend, because their social conditions militated against this. There is a lot of anecdotal evidence of people from disadvantaged areas feeling that they are not good enough to attend church.

3. The last century has seen an explosion of entertainment opportunities. From the 1870s onwards, the music hall and organized sport began to claim working-class allegiance. By 1905, there were 430 pubs in Lambeth, compared to 172 places of worship.[5] These developments only accelerated throughout the twentieth century. My grandmother grew up in the northern, industrial working-class town of Darlington, marrying a steelworker and living in a classic two-up, two-down terraced house, with an outside toilet and a cobbled back lane for coal deliveries. She was just a few months old when the local Methodist chapel first opened, and she attended it for over ninety years. It was the central feature of her life – not only her spiritual life, but also her social life. Apart from the pub, the chapel was the only regular source of entertainment. It was not that the chapel forsook its calling to proclaim the gospel in favour of entertainment. But the chapel was the centre of community life, so community life was focused around it. The result was that people were regularly exposed to Christian witness. But the growth of the cinema, and then television, spectator sports, the internet and a myriad other entertainment possibilities, means that churches no longer play this key role in working-class communities.

4. In some parts of evangelicalism, there has been a deliberate strategy to target people of influence. Many churches choose to reach students, at the expense of indigenous people on their doorsteps. Whatever the merits of this, it has meant that we have not poured resources into disadvantaged areas. Moreover, it can create an image of an ideal church or churchgoer that is far removed from the experience of working-class people.

5. The gospel often travels along relational lines. A Christian tells a friend about Jesus or invites a relative to an evangelistic event. Middle-class individuals typically have wide social networks that transcend geography. Working-class communities, by contrast, are still largely defined by neighbourhood. Friendship evangelism is great, but it does not enable the gospel to travel beyond our social networks, unless there are intentional attempts to build friendships with people who are not like us. John Mark Hobbins of London City Mission says, 'Many people live in networks which take precedence over their address, and many churches have grown because of this. But the reality for many people living in social housing or in cheaper housing is that their address is very likely to define their daily life.'[6]

6. A significant factor among converts is the phenomenon of 'social lift'. The gospel brings about change in people's lives: they stop drinking, care for their families, value literacy and education, work hard and save for the future. In time, this can make them – or their children – wealthier and perhaps less working class. David Bebbington says, 'There was a natural tendency for converted characters to gain skills, find regular employment and so rise out of the lowest ranks of society. Evangelical religion, as many commented at the time, was itself an avenue of upward social mobility.'[7]

Whatever the historical reasons, we are left with a situation in which working-class and deprived areas in the UK are not being reached with the gospel. There is a renewed concern among evangelicals for church planting, which is leading in turn to a growing concern to reach working-class people. As churches recognize areas in their locality with no gospel witness, they often identify areas of deprivation – areas with a social culture very different from their own. At the same time, Christians from such areas are beginning to make their voice heard.

In 2008, Steve Casey from Speke in Liverpool began canvassing opinion on how evangelicals could be encouraged to engage with the needs of working-class and deprived areas in the UK. This led to an informal working group of around fifteen to twenty practitioners, a mix of both Christian leaders who had grown up in deprived areas and middle-class Christians now ministering in such areas. The aim was to share issues and identify best practice. In 2009, Matt Banks organized a conference under the auspices of the South-East Gospel Partnership, with the title: 'Reaching the Unreached', which was held at St Helen's Bishopsgate in central London. This has now developed into an annual conference.

These two processes have merged to become 'Reaching the Unreached', an informal network of evangelical church leaders and church planters, mostly working in deprived areas (www.reachingtheunreached.org.uk).

The Reaching the Unreached working group includes:

- Matt Banks, studying at Oak Hill College
- Alan Black and John Mark Hobbins from London City Mission
- Efrem Buckle from Calvary Chapel, south London
- Steve Casey from Speke Baptist Church, Liverpool
- Duncan Forbes from New Life Church in Roehampton, south London

- Peter Froggatt from St Peter's Rock Ferry, Birkenhead on the Wirral
- Dai Hankey from Hill City Church in Trevethin, South Wales
- Andrew Holt from St Helen's Bishopsgate, London
- Pete Jackson from St Andrew's Kendray, Barnsley
- Jo McKenzie from Durham University, undertaking doctoral research into evangelicalism and social class
- Andy Mason from St John's, World's End, London
- Julian Rebera from New Life Church, Brighton
- Simon Smallwood from St George's Church, Dagenham
- Dan Strange, Lecturer in Culture, Religion and Public Theology at Oak Hill College
- Andy Toovey from Thirsty Church, Garndiffaith
- Myself, Tim Chester from The Crowded House, Sheffield

This book is the product of the working group. Our concern is not primarily to answer the question of *why* evangelicals should reach deprived areas, but to move on to explore *how* we can reach them. It arose from our consultations, the work of individuals within the group, the Reaching the Unreached blog (www.reachingtheunreached.org.uk) and my own work on this topic. It is common for authors to attribute the strength of a book to the contribution of other people, while taking responsibility for its weaknesses. This was never more true than with the present volume

In 1982, Roy Joslin published his landmark book, *Urban Harvest*.[8] It challenged evangelicals to reach working-class people and explored what this might look like. But that was 1982. Thirty years on, not only has working-class culture changed hugely, but, as we shall see, the category itself not longer does the job it once did.

Equally striking is the fact that nothing comparable has been written on this topic in the intervening years. The church in the West is awash with material on reaching postmoderns and engaging with postmodern culture. The theme seems almost ubiquitous, with a plethora of books, conferences, seminars and programmes. And all this is entirely appropriate. We need to engage with, and endeavour to identify, the appropriate apologetics for postmoderns. But the reality is that what is being addressed is largely a middle-class, professional or student culture.

Compared to this wealth of resources, it is striking how little there is on reaching working-class and deprived areas. This is not to say that nothing has been written on urban mission or mission among the poor. There are resources on the importance of this ministry, and resources on the necessity to address socio-economic needs. But there is very little on how to evangelize and disciple people in these areas, little on understanding their culture or contextualizing the gospel in their situation. Missional discussions on reaching deprived areas seem to stop at the observation that we need to run social projects.

Let me suggest three possible reasons why little has been written.

First, because the culture of the working class is generally a less literate culture, ministry in this context has not generated a body of literature, and lessons learned through experience have not been widely disseminated. In short, those producing theological reflection in written form are unlikely to be involved in coalface urban ministry, and those involved in urban ministry are unlikely to produce theological reflection in written form.

Secondly, it may reflect the suspicion with which social action has sometimes been regarded. The necessity to address social needs or focus on the marginalized has been the subject of much debate, and therefore of much literature. Those

committed to the urban poor have felt the need to defend that
focus. But there may be a danger that, in the process, we have
taken our eye off the evangelistic ball, so to speak.

One Christian worker, who used to run social projects on
an estate, realized that his group was not being gospel-centred.
Other Christians involved in 'good works' were confusing the
issue of the gospel in people's minds. For some groups, the
gospel is simply good works. Plenty of money goes to support
such groups, so that they are able to flyer the estate, hire staff
and so on. But gospel proclamation is missing.

Andy Mason, church planting in World's End, London, says
that the first things many middle-class Christians see on council
estates are the social problems. These capture our attention,
so we can think our role is to fix them. Of course, it is right
that we address them. But, he asks, what does God see? He
sees people for whom he sent his Son. Their fundamental
problem is not social policy, but sin. And the solution is not
gentrification, but Jesus.

Sharing our lives, serving the poor, blessing our neighbourhood, are all central to following Jesus. But social projects alone
are not enough. People are not 'saved' through these, but
through the gospel of Jesus Christ. Moreover, on its own,
social action is like a signpost pointing nowhere. Or worse still,
it points to our good works, and so reinforces people's innate
legalism. If people see us doing good among the poor, but do
not hear the message of divine grace, then, in all likelihood,
they will conclude that what we think is of utmost importance
is doing good, and assume we do good in order to make
ourselves right with God.[9]

Thirdly, we have often been wary of talking about the sins
of the poor. In our apologetic for urban ministry and social
involvement, we portray them as victims (which they are)
rather than sinners (which they also are). We downplay their

responsibility, and emphasize 'our' responsibility (the responsibility of the wider society of which we are a part). People
can even have somewhat romantic notions about the poor –
especially if their experience is largely secondary. I suspect this
is because we fear an argument that runs, 'It's their fault, so it's
not my responsibility.' But the problem with this argument
is not that the poor are faultless, but that the argument is
graceless. It is a basic tenet of the gospel that God's blessing
in our lives is not dependent on us being faultless. None of us
would have any hope, if that were the case. While fault may
shape the nature of our interventions, fault cannot become an
excuse for inaction – otherwise we deny the gospel we proclaim
and the grace on which we rely. We saw off the branch on which
we sit.

We want to affirm the renewed commitment to social
involvement. Indeed, my previous book, *Good News to the Poor*,[10]
presents the case for gospel-centred social action. We want to
affirm all that Christians are doing to transform communities,
both those working from the bottom up through community
development, and those working from the top down by influ-
encing political authorities or creating wealth.

But the focus of this book is on contextualized evangelism
(mission adapted to the context) and indigenized evangelism (mission led by local people). Bob Ekblad says,

> [Christians] are becoming more and more active in desperately
> needed ministries of service and presence, offering housing, soup
> kitchens, and clothing banks to the homeless and low-income.
> However, mainstream Christians are usually held back from (and
> even embarrassed about) sharing good news through Bible study,
> prayer, and one-on-one conversations about questions of faith . . .
> Mainstream Christians often support valuable programs that aim at
> helping the underclass 'catch up' with the mainstream. However,

most Christians are ill prepared for any kind of ministry of the Word
with those outside the institutional church . . . This must change!
The survival of the church is dependent on ordinary Christians
rediscovering good news in the Scriptures with and for others and
for themselves.[11]

We hope this book will inspire and equip people involved, or
interested in being involved, in working-class and deprived
areas. We cannot offer any sure-fire recipes for success. But we
do want you to feel this is a ministry that you can do and that
you will want to do.

Inevitably, the book presents generalizations. Generalizations are useful short cuts, but they are not universal descriptions
of everyone from a working-class or deprived background.
We are well aware that, while some things will resonate with
your experience, others will not. There are also other unreached
groups around us, such as first-generation immigrants and
people from a Muslim background, who require their own
contextual approaches. The focus of this book, however, is
on people – of all racial backgrounds – who live in working-
class and deprived areas.

Also, we have frequently observed that principles which are
important in working-class and deprived areas are also relevant
to middle-class churches. Many of the ideas in this book
will be true for middle-class contexts too. It may be that
ministry in deprived areas will, in turn, refresh our approaches
in middle-class areas.

Cari Crossley deserves special thanks for her work taking
notes during our consultations, gathering material and con-
ducting research visits to various churches.

The tagline of Grove booklets is: 'Not the last word, but
often the first'. It summarizes how I feel about this book. What
I offer here on behalf of the Reaching the Unreached team is

not the last word on the topic. But we do offer some principles and suggestions, in the hope that they will help those labouring in working-class and deprived areas, and in the hope that they will provoke a wider conversation.

Tim Chester
May 2012

1 CONTEXTUALIZATION IN WORKING-CLASS AND DEPRIVED AREAS

'There is an immense gulf between the Christian church and the working classes in this country,' declared Roy Joslin in his book, *Urban Harvest*, in 1982.[1] Although many of his observations about urban communities are still valid, it is notable how easily he uses the term 'working class' to describe urban people. He defines them as 'manual' workers, in 'trades' rather than professions, in locations such as 'factories, mills, mines, building sites, power stations, dockyards and other similar industrial locations'.[2]

Working-class culture in the twenty-first century

Reading Joslin's book in the twenty-first century, it is striking how clumsy the application of the term 'working class' now feels. Indeed, the nature of social class in the UK has since changed dramatically. Greater social mobility has made class distinctions harder to define. Many from working-class backgrounds have been to university and are now employed in white-collar jobs – traditional markers of middle-class identity. Yet many of these individuals continue to think of themselves as working class. Within the middle class, there is huge variation, encompassing professionals and tradespeople, Liberals and Conservatives, Socialists and free-marketeers, mixed together in all sorts of combinations. It would be hard, for example, to pin down a distinctly middle-class view on immigration, the scope of the state, sexuality, environmental issues, and so on. As David Cannadine's history of class in Britain shows, there is even a failure to agree whether class is a 'them-and-us' binary split between aristocrats and workers, a tripartite division of working, middle and upper classes, or a spectrum without clear distinctions.[3] We are left employing subcategories like 'lower middle' to find some kind of precision.

Yet, despite all this ambiguity, the categories of middle class and working class still shape social interaction in modern Britain. Like it or not, as soon as a person speaks, Brits tend to assign them to a social class and treat them accordingly. Stein Ringen says, 'What is peculiar to Britain is not the reality of the class system and its continuing existence, but class psychology: the preoccupation with class, the belief in class, and the symbols of class in manners, dress and language.'[4]

So the term 'working class' still has meaning, but the situation is more complex today than it was a generation ago.

Traditional employed working class
There is still what we might call a traditional working class: employed in manufacturing, socially conservative and with a strong collective identity.

Tom and Norah, well into their eighties, dance around the working men's clubs of West Yorkshire. Despite now owning their own home, they remain strident Labour supporters and unambiguously think of themselves as working class. Tea is at 4.30pm, and the front garden is manicured. Joan, a widow, knows everyone in her street. Every day, at 9am on the dot, she leaves her house to go to the newsagent, talking to people en route, before dropping off a newspaper at the home of a house-bound neighbour. Pete is a former postman. He's not the most garrulous person you'll meet, but outgoing enough to mow his neighbours' lawns and say 'hello'. He likes a pint down the pub or in his favourite armchair in front of the television.

Each of these working-class individuals feels tied to the people and geography of their local area. They feel part of something larger than themselves, be it the Labour Party, the trade union movement or the life of their neighbourhood. Significantly, though, all of these people are retired.

Wealthy self-employed working class
Some of yesterday's working-class people in the manufacturing industries, who joined trade unions and formed working men's clubs, have been replaced by today's builders, plumbers and electricians. There may be a paved driveway instead of a row of primulas in the front garden, and a flat-screen TV instead of the working men's club. They are not poor or marginalized. They don't feel the need to join trade unions, as they may even be their own boss. In many cases, they holiday in Spain instead of Blackpool. In some ways, they may look middle class, but their identity is still strongly working class.

Ethnic immigrants
Perhaps the closest match to the old style of British communal working classes can, perhaps somewhat ironically, be found in

the immigrant communities: Pakistanis with a fierce sense of family or Polish migrants helping one another into work. 'Everything turns on one person knowing another . . . It will never happen that a coach load of Poles can come over here and go to the job centre. It isn't like that. Everything is done on the basis of knowing someone.'[5]

Benefit class

The manufacturing industry, which sustained, and perhaps even defined, the working class, is now largely gone. Yet the estates and terraces built to support the mines, mills and assembly lines still remain, as do the high-rise flats that replaced urban slum tenements. And people remain, no longer in long-term jobs, but switching between short-term work and benefits. In some families, this partial unemployment has spanned generations. The line between employment and unemployment is often fluid, as the younger gener-ation routinely work for a few months before returning to benefits.

Popular myth suggests that there are many people who opt not to work, choosing instead to sponge off the state by living on benefits. It is a myth sustained by alarming anecdotes that capture the imagination. The statistics, however, do not bear this out. In 2000, there were 47,700 individuals who had claimed Jobseeker's Allowance for five years or more. By 2011 this was just 4,200 people.

> Research by LSE Professor John Hills shows low earners in the bottom 20% move in and out of insecure work in temporary jobs, never getting their foot on a ladder. The growth of agency work consigns willing workers to a life revolving through the job centre door . . . It is a miserable, underpaid culture of outsourced jobs with no future.[6]

Tax credits and housing benefits effectively subsidize employers who do not pay a living wage.

Another character of popular myth is the feckless, anti-social, aggressive 'chav'. Such people do exist, but in parts of the media they are made to represent working-class communities as a whole. Owen Jones calls this: 'the demonization of the working class'.[7] The word 'chav' itself is, as one Christian from a London estate put it to me, 'an abhorrent term that I find very offensive'. The reality is that the primary victims of anti-social behaviour are other inhabitants on council estates, many of whom lament the way such behaviour leads others to view their neighbourhood as less respectable.

> Lisa was incensed at the way that a minority ('newcomers') were 'letting the estate down' by giving it a bad image in the eyes of those high-class passers-by with the power to label a place as respectable or not . . . Linda felt ashamed to invite people back to her flat, both because of the estate's poor physical state and because her neighbours ('problem families') were 'shouting, banging the doors, ripping the rubbish when it's left outside the doors'.[8]

Citing research from the 1930s, Paul Watt says,

> The social history of council housing demonstrates that communal sociability was often undermined by antagonistic status divisions along lines of roughness and respectability . . . This rough/respectable distinction has proved to be an enduring element within the British working class, albeit one that has proved difficult to precisely pin down.[9]

In other words, distinctions within working-class communities are not new. But they do seem to have become more polarized and institutionalized in recent decades. This may be due to the collapse of manufacturing jobs and the shift to a service economy with low-paid casual employment. Another factor was the UK Government's 'right-to-buy' programme in the 1980s, which enabled wealthier tenants to buy their own homes. Prior to this, council estates contained a broad mix of people, many of whom were in long-term skilled employment. Now many of those who bought their own homes have moved on, leaving a diminishing quantity of public housing, concentrated towards those who are more marginalized or insecure. In Camden, for example, the percentage of households renting from the council with no-one in paid employment rose from 19% in 1967 to 62% in 1993. Council housing has become 'tenure of last resort'. 'This kind of stigmatizing "underclass" discourse, that conflates council renting with moral decline and criminality, dominates mass media and policy representation of council estates. Such representations have come to acquire a powerful mythic quality in the British social imagination . . . in which negative place images of social housing have congealed around immovable stigmatized reputations.'[10] Alessandra Buonfino and Geoff Mulgan summarize:

Working-class prestige and power was at its height in the years after 1945. Britain was still a rigidly hierarchical society, with strict rules of pronunciation, etiquette, appropriate dress and even the courting of marriage partners. But the middle-classes respected the working-classes as embodying the best patriotic values of stoical suffering and hard work. Today the respect of the rich for the poor has virtually disappeared, displaced by the dismissive language of 'chavs' and 'yobs', ASBOs and scroungers. The old white working-class is dismissed as racist and unreconstructed, while the newer working-classes from Asia and the Caribbean are seen as dangerous sources of crime or terrorism. At the same time, many areas of poor Britain have lost some of their own capacities to act. Where in the 1950s even the poorest areas contained people with experiences of leadership – foremen and shop stewards, for example – today there are many areas where there is no one with experience of comparable roles.[11]

The church has not done well at reaching the traditional working class, but there is an even greater chasm between the benefit culture and evangelical church culture. This gap includes clothes, accent, music and life experience. And it works both ways. A typical middle-class, evangelical Christian may struggle to respect the single mother who, she feels, relies too readily on the benefit system. But equally, the single mother may struggle to respect the Christian, who, she perceives, knows nothing of the realities of life and genuine hardship.

All of these groups – traditional working class, wealthier working class, immigrant communities and a less visible benefit class – are discernible in Simon Smallwood's description of Dagenham, where he is the minister of St George's Church:

> Until five years ago, it was hard-core, old Labour, white working class. Now it has had a huge influx of mostly West African economic migrants and is the happy hunting ground of the BNP. While the local population is enterprising and hard-working, and has greater cash wealth than ever before, the culture behind the front door has not changed much, and there is still a significant underclass who are just less visible. So all the usual marks of 'poverty' are still evident – low educational attainment, high crime, poor health, teenage pregnancy.

So the term 'working class' no longer describes all those who are not middle class, because it does not adequately describe the non-working benefit class, whose values differ in significant respects from those of traditional working-class culture. Yet it is hard to find an alternative term that is not derogatory. When asked how they would describe themselves, they often use a colloquial term that does not transcend their context. The English talk about 'council estates' and people 'from the estate', but Scots have 'housing schemes' and people 'from the scheme'. (Estates in Scotland are where you go to shoot grouse.) Neither formal terms like 'the marginalized', 'socially excluded', 'underclass', nor informal terms like 'street' or 'scally' quite do the job.

We have opted to avoid labelling people and instead allude to their geography, with the somewhat clumsy phrase: 'working-class and deprived areas'. Even 'deprived' can be pejorative, defining an area in terms of its deficiencies, without recognizing what is good. I remember, as a teenager, being involved in a church-twinning project. My middle-class church wanted to link up with a poor church, so we were interested in the local problems. But the members of the church were more interested in telling us what was good about their neighbourhood. This was their home, and they wanted to celebrate it.

What all these groups have in common, with the exception of the Afro-Caribbean community, is that they are largely unreached by the evangelical church.

Culture and contextualization

This is how a couple seeking to start a church on a council estate in Grantham, Leicestershire, described their experience:

> We started by reading lots of books on church planting and church models. We also began networking with a number of church planters. The lack of resources and information for reaching council estates was evident, and we have struggled to understand fully the mind and thinking of the people who live on the estate. Neither of us is from council estates, and we have experienced a stiff learning curve.

Culture is the air we breathe. It shapes our attitudes, speech, thinking, priorities, behaviour and relationships. Yet, most of the time, we are unaware of its influence. It is often the encounter with different cultures that first reveals to us our own culture. Entering another culture can be like playing a game without knowing the rules. What's more, there is no complete written record of the rules, and the other participants cannot tell you the rules, though they immediately know when you have broken one. Some people are reaching the area in which they grew up. They instinctively know its culture. But for others, reaching deprived areas is an exercise in cross-cultural ministry.

Here are six principles that shape a Christian view of culture:

1. God created cultures, and he delights in cultural variety

Culture and cultural diversity are good things. They are God's intention for the world. He gave humanity the command to fill the earth, and this has been commonly interpreted to include a mandate for cultural development and scientific endeavour. God's plan was for humanity to spread across the earth and, in so doing, develop diversity. Babel was not only a judgment on a society that was proud and evil, but a measure to force humanity to scatter as God had commanded, rather than come together as it had done. God forced upon humanity the diversity that he had planned, but which they had rejected.

2. Sin distorts cultures and creates cultural conflict

At the same time, every culture is corrupted by the fall, and there are elements within every culture that are sinful. Sinful actions become ingrained in culture, to the extent that they exert a strong hold. This is the power of 'the world' of which the New Testament speaks. This is why we are warned about worldliness (1 John 2:15–17), and this is why Paul says, 'Do not conform any longer to the pattern of this world, but be transformed by the renewing of your mind. Then you will be able to test and approve what God's will is – his good, pleasing and perfect will' (Romans 12:2).

3. The gospel both affirms and judges every culture
It is the tension between 'good, but fallen', between principles 1 and 2, that means we must be sensitive to local cultures, while also being committed to their transformation. The elements of any culture can be divided into those elements which:

- accord with the gospel and should be celebrated (e.g. community bonds and hard work)
- are neutral and can be used to express gospel truth (e.g. most musical styles)
- are sinful and should be challenged by the gospel (e.g. unbiblical attitudes to women)

All cultures contain this tension of good and sinful. The Lausanne Covenant says,

> Culture must always be tested and judged by Scripture (Mark 7:8, 9, 13). Because men and women are God's creatures, some of their culture is rich in beauty and goodness (Matt. 7:11; Gen. 4:21, 22). Because they are fallen, all of it is tainted with sin and some of it is demonic. The gospel does not presuppose the superiority of any culture to another, but evaluates all cultures according to its own criteria of truth and righteousness, and insists on moral absolutes in every culture.[11]

4. Christians should both affirm and transform cultures
We must be culturally sensitive. Every community has a past, a history, stories of success and failure. It has things of which

it is rightly proud. It has detailed knowledge of its locality. If we ignore such things, our work will be less effective and we will have negated an important resource of the community – its own heritage. But we must also be prepared to challenge culture. We cannot accept the postmodern assumption that all aspects of all cultures are valid.

5. The gospel transcends culture, without denying cultural differences
The gospel is transcultural. It unites people of different races and cultures, so that what unites them (Christ) is more important than what divides them (cultural diversity). Christian mission must witness to the reconciling nature of the gospel and the eschatological vision of people from every nation, tribe and tongue, gathered around the throne of the Lamb.

But we must also be careful how we express this transcultural dimension. The gospel is still to be expressed in culturally diverse ways. The danger is that those who are from a dominant culture can – often unwittingly – use talk of the transcultural nature of the gospel to impose their cultural norms on others. This means that often we will have to go out of our way to ensure that less dominant cultures are included, respected and expressed.

6. Missional engagement with culture is a two-way process
Clearly, we face the challenge of communicating the gospel into a culture. But we are also challenged by our engagement with culture. We, too, are shaped by our culture, with its good and bad elements. Culture is so much part of who we are that we often do not notice it. The rules are often subconscious, and we see other people's culture more clearly, because we notice the contrast with our norms. But we must recognize that often they are our norms and not gospel norms. Our

culture is not the norm from which other cultures deviate, or the ideal to which other cultures should aspire.

So the problem is that we are so immersed in our culture that we do not see it, let alone its defects. That is why missionary engagement with another culture is a two-way process. Our culture starts to come into focus, so that we can see it more clearly – good and bad – and how the gospel can enlighten and transform it. We read the Bible through the hermeneutical glasses of our own culture. But our engagement with the urban poor will expose our own cultural assumptions.

Contextualization in working-class areas and urban estates

So we have seen that all cultures contain within them elements that are:

- good – where they correspond to the gospel
- bad – where they conflict with the gospel
- indifferent – in which case, this very diversity is actually affirmed by the gospel

We cannot give a blanket *affirmation* of working-class culture. The gospel will challenge and transform some aspects. The result will be that converts will become 'less' working class. But neither can we make a blanket *condemnation* of working-class culture. There are many elements that conform to the gospel and are therefore affirmed by it. A blanket condemnation is what we issue only when we assume working-class people ought to become middle class. Ruby Payne says,

> Another notion among the middle class and educated is that, if the
> poor had a choice, they would live differently. The financial resources

would certainly help make a difference. Even with the financial resources, however, not every individual who received those finances would choose to live differently. There is a freedom of verbal expression, an appreciation of individual personality, a heightened and intense emotional experience, and a sensual, kinesthetic approach to life usually not found in the middle class or among the educated. These patterns are so intertwined in the daily life of the poor that to have those cut off would be to lose a limb. Many choose not to live a different life.[13]

The same principles, of course, apply to middle-class culture. It is neither wholly bad nor wholly good. It warrants neither blanket affirmation nor blanket condemnation.

> *It is a matter of moral indifference whether you prefer pie'n'peas or feta salad.*

There are also areas of indifference. It is a matter of moral indifference whether you prefer pie'n'peas or feta salad. Even here, though, the gospel celebrates this diversity among humanity as a fulfilment of God's intentions.

In the light of the above, we should expect the following:

- Working-class Christians should change (where their values conflict with the gospel). This will include changes in some areas that make them more middle class (where middle-class values correspond to the gospel). But we should not expect them to *become* middle class (because middle-class culture is not wholly good, and diversity is to be celebrated).
- Middle-class Christians should change (where their values conflict with the gospel). This will include changes in some areas that make them more working class (where working-class values correspond to the

gospel). But we should not expect them to *become* working class (because working-class culture is not wholly good, and diversity is to be celebrated).

We have already noted the phenomenon of 'social lift', of converts acquiring new attitudes and behaviours that lead to upward social mobility. To some extent, this reflects an aspiration by new Christians towards middle-class values, which, in turn, reflects the church culture into which they are socialized. In other words, social lift may be a genuine phenomenon, but it only creates middle-class people if middle-class values are seen as the norm to which one should aspire. As we've seen, some middle-class values may indeed reflect gospel norms, but not all do.

Moreover, social lift should be accompanied by a sacrificial and passionate desire to reach others. Why should such a lift equate to moving away from those in need, when we follow a Saviour who left the glory of heaven to come to the poverty of earth? Paul's default was to encourage people to remain where God had placed them (1 Corinthians 7:17–20). So, alongside the 'social lift' that comes from the gospel, we should expect a parallel phenomenon of 'social drop', in which people remain in, or move to, deprived areas. Social drop, too, is a product of the gospel. It arises because, through the gospel, people no longer live for career, comfort or security, but instead want to live generously and make it their ambition to 'preach the gospel where Christ [is] not known' (Romans 15:20).

In 2008, I spent a day with Carlos. Carlos had grown up in the ghettos of Chicago. His parents were drug addicts; his aunt was a witch. As we drove round the neighbourhood in which he had grown up, he identified the homes of drug dealers, pointed out gangs on street corners, showed me scenes of recent violence and crime. Carlos was converted through a Christian youth programme. He got an education, gained a degree and is now thinking of doing a PhD. He has a respectable job as a primary school teacher. He is happily married and owns his own home. But Carlos still lives in the ghetto. The school where he works and the church that he leads are in the ghetto. Social lift? Yes. A comfortable life in the suburbs? No.

Imbalanced mutual adaptation

What does all this mean for churches? Let me suggest a double principle that can be summarized by the phrase: 'imbalanced mutual adaptation'. These two principles apply wherever different cultures come together within the Christian community, but we will apply them specifically to working-class and middle-class differences.

The first aspect is that of 'mutual adaptation'. In other words, within the life and mission of the church, there needs to be mutual adaptation. Both working-class and middle-class people need to adapt to take account of one another.

Secondly, that mutual adaptation should be 'imbalanced'. The dominant culture within the wider society needs to adapt more, in this case middle-class Christians. Without this intentionality, *the dominant culture in society will dominate in the church*. The gospel transcends culture, but this does not mean that it creates some kind of culture-less church. It is not simply a question of numbers. Middle-class culture is the dominant culture, not because it is the majority culture, but because it is the culture of success, power and authority. So, without imbalanced adaptation, the working class will defer to the middle class, because this is how everyone is used to things functioning, and middle-class cultural mores will be seen as the norm. Leaders will be middle class because leadership in the world is largely middle class, and therefore being middle class is woven into our expectations of leadership. So we need to make a special effort.

What you project from the front in corporate gatherings is very important, so expressing diversity in your gatherings matters. The one who stands at the front is modelling the kind of church you are, or aspire to be. The images, language and cultural references will be important.

This principle of imbalanced mutual adaptation is perhaps just a pretentious way of articulating what the New Testament describes in terms of love and forbearance:

> As a prisoner for the Lord, then, I urge you to live a life worthy of the calling you have received. Be completely humble and gentle; be patient, bearing with one another in love. Make every effort to keep the unity of the Spirit through the bond of peace.
> (Ephesians 4:1–3)

> Do nothing out of selfish ambition or vain conceit, but in humility consider others better than yourselves. Each of you should look not only to your own interests, but also to the interests of others. Your attitude should be the same as that of Christ Jesus . . .
> (Philippians 2:3–5)

So how are middle-class values reflected in evangelicalism?

- We value professionalism
- Our programmes reflect a diarized schedule and the importance of punctuality
- We are reserved and suspicious of enthusiasm and passion
- University education is seen as a moral good and a primary means of self-improvement
- We assume our leaders need to be university-educated

What does it mean for middle-class Christians to contextualize or adapt to working-class or deprived areas? There is obviously no substitute for living among a people. But should we act as if we are working class or poor? I think not. That would be inauthentic, and people would see straight through us. When Paul said he was 'all things to all men' (in 1 Corinthians 9), he did not mean that he pretended to be a Gentile. He meant that he adapted to reach Gentiles, not expecting them, for example, to adhere to the Mosaic law. The overriding principle was service: 'Though I am free and belong to no man, I make myself a slave to everyone, to win as many as possible' (verse 19). Paul's actions were governed by his desire to reach others with the gospel: 'I do all this for the sake of the gospel, that I may share in its blessings' (verse 23).

Consider my attitude to my teenage children. I don't pretend to be fourteen. My teenagers would not take very kindly to that! It would be embarrassing and patronizing. But I do take an interest in what interests them and spend time with them, doing what they enjoy doing. I communicate in ways they will understand.

Andy Mason says,

> You need to adapt without being fake. The key thing is to come with a servant heart and a commitment to love others. If that's your attitude, then you'll find that people stop being 'other'. They stop being black or white or Muslim or working class, and instead they become friends. And then what happens is that you begin to change, and it's not affected change, but the natural influence of friends.

So, while middle-class Christians should not pretend to be working class, they should make radical and sacrificial changes to remove any trappings that hinder gospel communication or

create unnecessary barriers to belief. Citing Geoffrey Wilson,
Roy Joslin says of Paul,

> 'A study of Paul's sermons in the Acts of the Apostles shows that
> he adapted his presentation of the gospel to suit the particular
> needs of his listeners. The apostle was always careful to take
> account of differences in national character and cultural
> development (or the lack of it) . . . ' In recognising the working-
> classes as a definable group of people within today's society, we
> are following a biblical principle . . . Middle-class values are different
> from (and not superior to) working-class values . . . The content of
> the language Paul used [in Acts 14:8–18 and Acts 17:16–31] was
> determined by Scripture; the form of the language used was
> governed by local culture.[14]

Today, Pete Jackson, in Kendray, Barnsley, is leading a midweek
home Bible study on Hebrews 6. He himself reads the passage
aloud, to avoid embarrassing anyone who might struggle to
read. The group then pray together, trying to use the passage
to shape their prayers. A number are related in one way or
another. Family ties are strong on the estate, with few people
moving away.

St John's Church on World's End estate in London has a
gym on site to connect with men who would never otherwise
consider attending church. 'We have created male space in the
church,' comments Andy Mason. 'Women often do face-to-
face relationships, but men do side-by-side. So they'll talk while
doing weights or working on a common project. They appre-
ciate you telling them straight what the Bible says, but shy
away from emotional disclosure. They respect it when there is
a sense of your being on their side.'

New Life Church in Roehampton meets in a youth club on
the estate. Tea and toast are available as people gather. The

meeting begins with someone reading a psalm and praying. The congregation has used pre-recorded, well-known Christian songs, overlaid with a hip-hop beat, but increasingly they are writing their own songs, because they want their praise to reflect indigenous styles and express an indigenous theology. Duncan Forbes, the church leader, typically preaches using verse-by-verse exposition, with illustrations drawn on a flipchart or enacted in front of the congregation. His style is direct and passionate, with immediate language and examples, and his talk includes some interaction with the congregation. After the meeting, many of the congregation will go back to Duncan and Shay's flat for lunch.

One day in Joppa, Simon Peter had an extraordinary vision from God that turned his whole world upside down. He was converted. Not to a personal, living faith in Jesus Christ. Not to a faith which drove him to witness boldly to others. Not to a faith for which he was prepared to die. For, by most of our standards, Simon Peter was already a hero of the faith. He already knew the power of the gospel in his life and had witnessed with authority to the risen Lord Jesus. Yet, despite all this, it took another work of God to show him the full reach of the gospel, to convert him to culture-transcending mission.

While Peter was praying, he became hungry and, in his vision, saw a sheet being let down from heaven. It was full of animals which, by Jewish standards, were unclean.

> Then a voice told him, 'Get up, Peter. Kill and eat.' 'Surely not, Lord!' Peter replied. 'I have never eaten anything impure or unclean.' The voice spoke to him a second time, 'Do not call anything impure that God has made clean.' This happened three times, and immediately the sheet was taken back to heaven.
>
> (Acts 10:13–16)

While Peter was wondering what all this meant, a delegation from Cornelius arrived. Now Cornelius was a God-fearing, generous Gentile from Caesarea. He too had a seen a vision, and, in it, God had told him to send men to Joppa to seek out Peter. The Spirit told Peter to accept Cornelius's invitation. Peter made the men his guests before accompanying them to Caesarea. He was now beginning to comprehend his vision. He told the gathering that Cornelius assembled, 'You are well aware that it is against our law for a Jew to associate with a Gentile or visit him. But God has shown me that I should not call any man impure or unclean' (Acts 10:28). When Cornelius told Peter of his vision, Peter said, 'I now realise how true it is that God does not show favouritism but accepts men from every nation who fear him and do what is right' (Acts 10:34–35). Peter preached the gospel message of the Spirit-empowered life of Jesus, his death on the cross, his resurrection, and the promise of

Before Cornelius could be converted, Peter had to be converted.

forgiveness through his name. 'While Peter was still speaking these words, the Holy Spirit came on all who heard the message . . . Then Peter said, "Can anyone keep these people from being baptised with water? They have received the Holy Spirit just as we have"' (Acts 10:44, 46–47).

Before Cornelius could be converted, Peter had to be converted. Of course, he knew the gospel would go to the nations (Luke 24:45–47). But he assumed that the Gentiles would first have to become like the Jews. Jews becoming like Gentiles was unthinkable.

Whose conversion involves the greatest struggle? Peter, the Christian, who argues with God three times, saying 'Surely not, Lord!' Or by contrast, a whole room full of Gentiles receiving the Holy Spirit as soon as they hear the message and offering themselves for baptism. Peter, representing the majority Christian culture, is most resistant to change. And this change, when it happens, results in criticism from his peers (Acts 11:1–3).

For most of us in the UK, it is not the ethnic prejudices of a Peter that constrain our mission, but the prejudices of social class and race. Many of us who are middle class may need to be converted to culture-transcending mission before we can reach the unreached. Those of us who are working class may need to be converted to a culture-transcending church before we can work together in mission. Peter's prejudices were laid out on the sheet that was lowered from heaven. What would be laid out on your sheet?

2 THE CULTURE OF WORKING-CLASS AND DEPRIVED AREAS

What does a black teenage girl in London have in common with a retired coal miner in Doncaster? As we have seen, describing the culture of working-class and deprived areas is far from straightforward, because, in reality, there are cultures (plural) of working-class and deprived areas, rather than one single culture. There are the traditional working-class and the benefit cultures, and to these we can add: ethnic differences; age-related subcultures; northern and southern differences; Scottish, Irish, N. Irish, Welsh and English identities; and urban, rural and suburban cultures.

The strengths and limitations of contextualization

This, however, does not mean that it is pointless to outline some common characteristics of the culture of working-class and deprived areas. Indeed, identifying the culture of any group and contextualizing to that culture can be a helpful process, as long as two important truths are borne in mind.

First, every culture is part of a common humanity. Whatever the distinguishing characteristics, people within that culture have characteristics that are true of everyone. They are made in God's image, an image that they still reflect to some degree, by God's common grace, even though that image is now marred by sin. They enjoy the goodness of God's world and long for the relationships for which they were made. They are all broken people, sinners who face the judgment of God, and they are the victims of the sins of others.

Secondly, every person is a unique individual. Whatever the distinguishing characteristics of a particular culture, people within it have aspects of personality and interests that are unique to them. They may be a truck driver who likes opera or an unemployed teenager who loves reading. Each person is different and part of a matrix of relationships that is unique to them. So, while cultural descriptions may be commonly true, we cannot assume they are true of the person in front of us. *We need to contextualize on a person-by-person basis.*

You can see this through the following diagram.

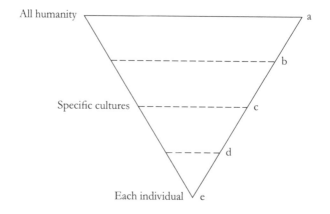

Everyone is both part of our common humanity ('a') and a unique individual ('e'). In between these two realities, we can slice the triangle at different points, thereby including varying numbers of people. We can, for example, slice it at point 'c' and describe the culture of people from working-class and deprived areas. This would produce some useful descriptions that would be generally true of people from this culture, though we must remember that everyone is different and not all our generalizations will be true all the time. Or we can take a broader cultural group, such as British people ('b'). Here we can identify some generalizations that are true of both working-class and middle-class Brits. Or we can take a narrow slice at point 'd' and describe the culture of urban rap music or northern working men's clubs.

Three implications follow.

First, we need to remain confident that the gospel is 'the power of God for the salvation of everyone who believes' (Romans 1:16). Everyone is part of our common humanity ('a'), sharing a common identity as God's image-bearers, facing the common problems of human sin and divine judgment, and needing a common Saviour. Whatever marks out a particular culture as different, everyone needs the gospel and everyone can find in the gospel the hope of salvation.

Secondly, we must always treat people as people, not in an undifferentiated way as generic representatives of a social class. We cannot let our cultural analysis harden into presuppositions or prejudices. It is important to heed the warning of one gospel worker on a council estate in Sheffield: 'I struggle with some of the material that is produced to try to help people in this area, as I think it often generalizes people too much.'

Thirdly, generalized cultural descriptions are helpful tools, because often they speed up the process of person-specific contextualization, and there are sufficient common cultural characteristics to make contextualization worth pursuing. Whatever the differences among people from working-class and deprived areas, they do not invalidate the process of considering their common traits. The French are heterogeneous, but it is still useful for missionaries to France to learn about French history and think about contextualizing to French culture. In the same way, working-class and deprived areas are heterogeneous, but it is still worthwhile for those working in these areas to think about contextualizing.

So we can helpfully describe specific cultures, as long as we remember both: (a) that every individual is unique – in some respect like no-one else; and (b) part of a common humanity – in some respects like everyone else.

So, in the light of the above, in this chapter we will identify:

1. some common characteristics of people from working-class and deprived areas (level 'c' in the diagram);
2. some tools to help people undertake their own context-specific cultural analysis (level 'd' in the diagram).

Common characteristics of working-class and deprived areas

1. Anti-authoritarianism

People from the above areas often have few positive experiences of authority. They may come from families where parental authority is dysfunctional or they may have had negative experiences at school and work. Their experience of the state is likely to be either that of threat or an unwieldy bureaucracy. Parents often side with their children against teachers. Many will have experienced crime without redress, which, in turn, blurs attitudes towards criminality. 'If an individual is in generational poverty, organized society is viewed with distrust, even distaste. The line between what is legal and illegal is thin and often crossed.'[1] They do not recognize the category of 'loving authority'. This makes relating to God as Lord difficult. It means that the proclamation of the kingdom or government of God is not heard as good news.

2. Entitlement mentality

The benefit system has created many people who are used to others providing for them. Need equals expectation: someone will meet that need. So they can easily see the church as another 'service-provider'. Talk of 'caring for one another' can be interpreted in terms of entitlement.

3. Reputation

People in these areas often define themselves by their place in the social strata. It is of utmost importance to be somebody, to be respected. People are happy when there is equality, but, when someone has more than you, then you 'need' what they have. Reputation is everything. So, for example, some people from such areas will avoid using charity or thrift shops. Identity is linked to appearance, so you avoid buying second-hand clothes. Among the middle class, in contrast, identity is tied to education, achievement and worldview.

4. The struggle

Struggle is a major theme in the life of many people from the above areas. It is not just that life is hard, but the fact of struggling forms part of their identity. Indeed, they interpret their lives in terms of this struggle. Problems are part of 'the struggle', part of what it means to be a person in a deprived area. The identity of the enemy or oppressor may vary, but, in general terms, it is the struggle against the system or against

48

UNREACHED

mentality and low aspirations.

5. Victim mantality

People often see themselves as victims, with little power over
their lives. Because they feel powerless, they may resist the
system by being passive-aggressive rather than aggressive in a
combative way.

This victim mentality means that any failings in my life are
the failings of other people. Shame is not so much a concern
for the wrong done to others, but the inability to be the person
I want to be, or to accept the person I am. As a result, any talk
of guilt is seen as an attack on me. So, even when you highlight
my guilt, I can still see myself as the victim.

This is not to deny that people are victims. But we must
encourage them not to make victimhood their identity. Victimhood can be attractive because it allows individuals to avoid
responsibility for their actions. But only true repentance will
lead to forgiveness and freedom, and repentance only comes
when people take responsibility for their sin.

6. Limited aspirations

Middle-class lives are more likely than working-class lives to see
hope for change. Not always, of course, because many middle-
class people also struggle with depression and other issues. But
middle-class individuals are more likely to believe that, if they
work hard, then they can succeed. Models of success abound.
But those from deprived areas see little prospect of change. To
have ambitions is to set yourself up for a fall or to have pretensions. So there is an underlying fatalism. 'People don't want to
take the risk of a new job or a venture because they know in
their hearts that they will probably fail.'[2]

This, in turn, creates a strong tendency to live in the moment.

Saving or preparing for the future is seen as pointless. There is a high premium on entertainment, with little sense of deferred gratification.

7. Relational assets

Traditionally, within mining communities, if a husband died, colleagues and neighbourhoods would take up a collection for the widow, often raising large sums of money. This social solidarity was evident during the miners' strike of the 1980s. Now, however, working-class institutions, like trade unions and working men's clubs, are in decline.

Yet social solidarity persists at a personal level. There is almost an unwritten contract that you share what you have with friends. Human assets matter more than financial assets. Friends help friends. 'There's a close bond on housing schemes,' says Mez McConnell. '[Friends are] there for the long term.' Ruby Payne says,

> One of the hidden rules of poverty is that any extra money is shared. Middle-class puts a great deal of emphasis on being self-sufficient. In poverty, the clear understanding is that one will never get ahead, so when extra money is available, it is either shared or immediately spent. There are always emergencies and needs; one might as well enjoy the moment. [A poor person with money] will share the money; she has no choice. If she does not, the next time she is in need, she will be left in the cold. It is the hidden rule of the support system. In poverty, people are possessions, and people can rely only on each other. It is absolutely imperative that the needs of an individual come first. After all, that is all you have – people.[3]

Steve Casey from Speke in Liverpool says,

> We thought we would create community. But the locals know more about community. Our youth work could not compete with the

strength of community in the area. If someone owes their last £10 for rent, and a friend asks for £10, then they will give it to the friend. If people are under sanction at work for attendance, they would rather lose their job than miss a distant relative's funeral.[4]

8. Non-abstract, concrete thinking

Our education systems condition people to think in terms of abstract principles, axioms and sequences. But working-class people are likely to organize knowledge in more relational ways. It is all about making connections with existing learning. These individuals are interested in what works – in the practical and immediate. For example, they are less likely to contribute to prayer meetings when the call to pray is general, but they will happily pray for specific requests. This does not mean they are illogical, but rather that their logic is expressed in concrete terms. They are more likely to express thought in pictures and stories.

Such people typically learn more through kinesthetic models, that is, learning by doing rather than by listening. They learn best when their learning builds upon prior learning, when they are able to contribute their own existing knowledge, and when they can connect what they are learning to that existing knowledge. They learn with rather than from people. The opinion of friends matters more than the opinion of 'authorities'. They find out information by asking someone rather than looking it up in a book. Many have been disenfranchised by formal education. This means that an interactive Bible study with a focus on analysing the text can easily feel like an English comprehension exercise. So such people will often prefer sermons to Bible studies.

9. Non-diarized, relational lifestyles

The working class generally live in the 'now'. They do not make appointments or feel any great obligation to keep appointments. The currency of the poor is relationships (what is known as 'social capital'). Your allegiance is to the people you are with, not to the clock. 'Your schedule must change,' says Mez McConnell. 'If you meet someone, go with the flow. Being missional can't be fitted into a diary slot. Middle-class people dislike the chaos of the housing scheme, so they try to impose order on it.' He advocates 'scheduled spontaneity' – setting aside time to hang out with other people.

The following summaries are from the work of Ruby Payne, an American educationalist, quoted earlier, whose analysis of generational poverty has been highly influential. Although written from a North American context, they largely resonate with experience in the UK, and summarize an academic perspective on the issues. Payne identifies key characteristics of what she calls 'generational poverty', long-term poverty that spans the generations. The UK equivalent would be families in which few from the different generations have had experience of long-term work. The second table highlights distinctive features of this culture, by contrasting their 'hidden rules' with those of other social classes.

Characteristics of generational poverty[5]

Background noise: Almost always, the TV is on, no matter what the circumstances. Conversation is participatory, often with more than one person talking at a time.

Importance of personality: Individual personality is what one brings to the setting – because money is not brought. The ability to entertain, tell stories and have a sense of humour is highly valued.

Significance of entertainment: When one can merely survive, then respite from survival is important. In fact, entertainment brings respite.

Importance of relationships: One only has people upon whom to rely, and those relationships are important to survival. One often has favourites.

Matriarchal structure: The mother has the most powerful position in the society, if she functions as a caretaker.

Oral-language tradition: Casual register is used for everything.

Survival orientation: The discussion of academic topics is generally not prized. There is little room for the abstract. Discussions centre on people and relationships. A job is about making enough money to survive, not about a career (e.g. 'I was looking for a job when I found this one').

Identity tied to lover/fighter role for men: The key issue for males is to be a 'man'. The rules are rigid, and a man is expected to work hard physically – and be a lover and a fighter.

Identity tied to rescuer/martyr role for women: A 'good' woman is expected to take care of, and rescue, her man and her children as needed.

Importance of non-verbal/kinesthetic communication: Touch is used to communicate, as are space and non-verbal emotional information.

Ownership of people: People are possessions. There is a great deal of fear and comment about leaving the culture and 'getting above your raisings'.

Negative orientation: Failure at anything is the source of stories and numerous belittling comments.

Discipline: Punishment is about penance and forgiveness, not about change.

Belief in fate: Destiny and fate are the major tenets of the belief system. Choice is seldom considered.

Polarized thinking: Options are hardly ever examined. Everything is polarized; it is one way or the other. These kinds of statements are common: 'I quit' and 'I can't do it.'

Mating dance: The mating dance is about using the body in a sexual way and verbally and sub-verbally complimenting body parts. If you have few financial resources, the way you sexually attract someone is with your body.

Time: Time occurs only in the present. The future does not exist, except as a word. Time is flexible and not measured. Time is often assigned on the basis of its emotional significance and not as actual measured time.

Sense of humour: A sense of humour is highly valued, as entertainment is one of the key aspects of poverty. Humour is almost always about people – either situations that people encounter or things people do to other people.

Lack of order/organization: Many of the homes/apartments of people in poverty are unkempt and cluttered. Devices for organization (files, planners, etc.) simply don't exist.

Lives in the moment – does not consider future ramifications: Being proactive, setting goals and planning ahead are not a part of generational poverty. Most of what occurs is reactive. Future implications of present actions are seldom considered.

Hidden rules among classes[6]			
	POVERTY	**MIDDLE CLASS**	**WEALTH**
POSSESSIONS	People	Things	One-of-a kind objects, legacies, pedigrees
MONEY	To be used, spent	To be managed	To be conserved, invested
PERSONALITY	Is for entertainment. Sense of humour is highly valued	Is for acquisition and stability. Achievement is highly valued	Is for connections. Financial, political, social connections are highly valued
SOCIAL EMPHASIS	Social inclusion of people he/she likes	Emphasis is on self-governance and self-sufficiency	Emphasis is on social exclusion
FOOD	Key question: Did you have enough? Quantity important	Key question: Did you like it? Quality important	Key question: Was it presented well? Presentation important
CLOTHING	Clothing valued for individual style and expression of personality	Clothing valued for its quality and acceptance into norm of middle class	Clothing valued for its artistic sense and expression. Designer important

Hidden rules among classes (*cont.*)

	POVERTY	MIDDLE CLASS	WEALTH
TIME	Present most important. Decision made for moment, based on feelings or survival	Future most important. Decisions made against future ramifications	Traditions and history most important. Decisions made partially on basis of tradition and decorum
EDUCATION	Valued and revered as abstract, but not as reality	Crucial for climbing success ladder and making money	Necessary tradition for making and maintaining connections
DESTINY	Believes in fate. Cannot do much to mitigate chance	Believes in choice. Can change future with good choices now	Noblesse oblige
LANGUAGE	Casual register. Language is about survival	Formal register. Language is about negotiation	Formal register. Language is about networking
FAMILY STRUCTURE	Tends to be matriarchal	Tends to be patriarchal	Depends on who has money
WORLDVIEW	Sees world in terms of local setting	Sees world in terms of national setting	Sees world in terms of international view

Hidden rules among classes *(cont.)*			
	POVERTY	**MIDDLE CLASS**	**WEALTH**
LOVE	Love and acceptance conditional, based upon whether individual is liked	Love and acceptance conditional, and based largely upon achievement	Love and acceptance conditional, and related to social standing and connections
DRIVING FORCES	Survival, relationships, entertainment	Work, achievement	Financial, political, social connections
HUMOUR	About people and sex	About situations	About social faux pas

Initial implications

In subsequent chapters, I will propose practical models of evangelism and discipleship that are adapted to people from this kind of culture (though, in many cases, they will turn out to be applicable to people from all backgrounds). In the meantime, here are some initial implications.

Passion

We need to be people with passion. Our education system promotes dispassionate 'objectivity'. Personal engagement with a subject is viewed with suspicion. Middle-class people tend to value cool and rational arguments. But people from working-class and deprived areas judge authenticity by a passionate engagement with truth. Working-class people want to see tears, excitement, conviction. We need to show how the truth impacts on our lives and emotions. One convert from a deprived area notes that members of his university church do not like a preacher who shouts, but people on the estate where he grew up do want to see passion. Martyn Lloyd-Jones, the well-known twentieth-century preacher, comments,

> Of all the people I have read of in the course of history I know of no people who have such a responsibility at the bar of eternal judgment as the people from roughly 1850 until today. The change took place somewhere in the 1850s. Until then the great impact of the Evangelical Revival of the eighteenth century still persisted and there had been other revivals and people knew about the power of the Holy Spirit. But suddenly we all became so respectable and so learned and people said, 'Ah, that old preaching is no longer good enough, the people are now receiving education. They are beginning to read and becoming learned and so on.' And the middle classes were becoming prosperous and wealthy. Then followed the most devastating thing that has afflicted the life of the church – Victorianism. It entered into the churches, particularly the Free Churches, which now began to imitate other forms of worship and the great word became 'dignity'. Dignity! Formality! Learning! Culture![7]

A. D. Gilbert says, 'The tendency towards professionalization and institutional order gradually altered the essential character of the Wesleyan movement during the period between 1791, when John Wesley died, and the 1840s.'[8] Wesley himself, describing his use of open-air preaching, said, 'I submitted to be more vile.'[9] Roy Joslin comments,

> Patterns of worship, methods of evangelism, the respective roles of ministry and laity were all deeply affected by this trend towards formalisation. As these changes came, church life generally

became more a matter of organisation than organism. The
preoccupation with 'order, respectability and style' tended to
accentuate the gap between the Nonconformist churches and
the social groups from which their members had formerly been
recruited.[10]

There were, of course, some notable exceptions. Charles
Haddon Spurgeon's preaching was described as 'redolent of
bad taste, vulgar, and theatrical'. Spurgeon replied, 'I am
perhaps vulgar, but it is not intentional, save that I must and
will make people listen. My firm conviction is that we have had
quite enough polite preaching, and many require a change.'[11]
Spurgeon's preaching drew thousands each week, many from
a working-class background. Spurgeon also established
orphanages, almshouses, and a pastors' college specifically for
men with limited formal education. By his death, the college
had trained close to 1,000 students, many of whom went on
to plant churches in the slums of London. Today, Pente-
costalism, with its passionate, exuberant meetings, is the branch
of Christianity having the greatest impact on people in disadvantaged areas.

Openness and forthrightness
We need to be people who are open about our struggles.
Outward respectability and a 'stiff upper lip' may be appropriate if you are the vicar of an upper-middle-class church.
But it will probably alienate you from a working-class congregation who will assume you have nothing to say into their life
experiences.

Church people can sometimes appear condescending or
patronizing. This happens when we try to be compassionate
or understanding, but still feel superior. Often the problem is
not with the content of what we say, but the attitude behind

it. My observation is that those who are most effective at reaching the poor often say it as it is. People respect this forthrightness, when the underlying disposition of the heart is shaped by grace.

People in deprived areas often see the world in black-and-white terms. They will take you literally. People interpret, 'Ring me any time' as giving them permission to phone you at two in the morning. But you can also readily tap into this worldview. People will not be fazed if you give them a straight answer to a question like, 'Will people go to hell?'

Lament

One specific form of discourse is common in deprived areas: lament. I was talking with someone who describes herself as 'from the street'. She said, 'We start by moaning to one another.' Christians can interpret this as ungodly grumbling. Of course, it may be that it is, but often little is meant by it. Indeed, perhaps we can use the structures of moaning, by associating it with the biblical category of lament. We can declare that we live in a fallen world. We can declare what is wrong with the world. And perhaps we can then begin to declare hope for that sinful world.

Storytelling

People from a working-class or disadvantaged area generally engage in discourse through storytelling rather than through asking personal questions. In working-class culture, information is volunteered rather than being 'demanded' through questions. Working-class people will quickly interpret questions as interrogation. A working-class person and a middle-class person meet and the middle-class person concludes, 'They weren't interested in me because they didn't ask me any personal questions.' The working-class person concludes,

'They don't trust me because they always interrogate me.' This culture of anecdotes means that gospel truth can be parcelled up in personal stories. Throwing out snippets of testimony is culturally appropriate and effective.

Food

Our eating habits are more culturally defined than many of us realize. Hospitality is a staple part of evangelical church culture, and we connect with people by offering them tea with homemade cake, or inviting them round for a meal. But people from working-class and deprived areas are often resistant to eating in someone else's home. Neighbours who routinely help one another out rarely eat a meal together. Homes often don't have dining tables, sometimes because of insufficient space, sometimes because food is eaten in front of the television. To accept hospitality from a middle-class person is to risk social embarrassment.

Recognizing that local taste is for plain 'honest' food, Pete Jackson's church on a northern council estate served pie and peas at their pool night. People enjoyed coming, but most wouldn't eat. The price, at £1.50, was not the problem, as people spend more than that on the lager they bring. Nor is the food the problem, as people happily take home any leftovers. But there seems to be some dynamic based around eating food with others in public.

Hospitality is a biblical imperative, so new believers may need to be challenged to transform their culture. But it is also important to recognize existing patterns of 'doing' food. Perhaps a late-night kebab or trip to the chippie or a drink in the pub is the way to share food with others. Or perhaps food is done in a less scheduled manner, offered on an ad hoc basis when someone happens to be in your home, rather than through an invitation to supper at 8pm on Friday.

Getting to know your neighbourhood

Remember what we said earlier. The broad characteristics of the culture of working-class and deprived areas are best treated as short cuts to understanding your area and the people within it, rather than as definitive guides. They will need to be tested and refined on a neighbourhood-by-neighbourhood and person-by-person basis. Not all will be true or valid in every respect in your context. Certainly not all will be true of all the people in your context.

So it is important to gain an understanding of your own context. Don't come into an area thinking that you know it all or understand it all. Expect that your first six months will probably not be a time of great ministry, but a time for you to learn and absorb. Daniel and Grace Howson spent two days a week during the first year just trying to get to know the area of Grantham that they wanted to reach. Every aspect of ministering in deprived contexts takes time. If you are not a 'native', you will be viewed with suspicion. Time may not make you fully part of the tribe, but you will gain a certain amount of respect if you are seen to be consistent under pressure and committed. And it will take time to get to know people and to learn what earns respect.

Think about the following questions and consider specific people you know. Thinking of concrete examples is always more helpful than defaulting to stereotypes.

- How do men and women dress?
- How and where do friends and family relate to one another?
- Who are the key models?
- To what music do people listen?
- How do people describe themselves, and with what social group do they identify?

- How far will people travel to work/shop/visit friends and family?
- What three activities do people spend most time doing?
- What is a typical home like?
- What proportion of people are employed? What jobs do they do?
- How are gender roles worked out?
- What do people most like about the culture?
- What do people most dislike about the culture?

If you are an insider, ask outsiders what it is they find strange about your neighbourhood. If you are an outsider, ask insiders how they view their neighbourhood. Try to view your area as would a taxi driver, a long-term resident, a member of an ethnic minority, and so on.

In *The Radical Reformission*, Mark Driscoll says,[12]

During the week, make an effort to learn from the people whom you encounter in public settings, such as the bank teller or grocery store clerk. Simply ask them what they've learned about people after interacting with so many. You will find they are a wealth of insight . . . Most importantly, speak with lost people who are not like you, not for the purpose of converting them but rather for the purpose of learning what life is like for them in their culture.

Where do people spend their time and money?

What do people do during their free time?

What do they fear?

What do they dream about?

Where do they shop?

What cultural experiences do they value?

What are the most painful experiences they have had?

What music do they listen to?

What film and television do they watch?

What do they find humorous?

In what ways are they self-righteous?

What do they read?

What is their spirituality?

Whom do they trust? Why?

What do they think about the gospel?

What sins will the gospel first confront and heal for these people?

The following questions may help identify opportunities for mission:

Where?[13]

- Where are the missional spaces (places and activities where you meet people)?
- Where do people experience community?
- Are there existing social networks with which you can engage, or do you need to find new ways of creating community within a neighbourhood?
- *Where* should you be in order to have missional opportunities?

When?

- When are the missional moments?
- What are the rhythms of your neighbourhood?
- How do people organize their time?
- What cultural experiences and celebrations do people value? How might these be used as bridges to the gospel?
- *When* should you be available to have missional opportunities?

What?

- What are people's fears, hopes and hurts?
- What 'gospel' stories are told in the neighbourhood?

What gives people identity (creation)? How do they
account for what's wrong with the world (fall)? What's
the solution (redemption)? What are their hopes
(consummation)?

- What barriers, beliefs or assumptions cause people to
  dismiss the gospel?
- What sins will the gospel first confront and heal for
  these people?
- In what ways are people self-righteous?
- What is the good news in this neighbourhood?
- What will church look like for residents in this
  neighbourhood?

These are some questions you might ask on first encountering
a new community or neighbourhood. But they should also be
questions we ask all the time, so that missional reflection
becomes a normal part of our life.

Barriers and bridges
A great way to organize your observations is to think in terms
of barriers and bridges to the gospel.

Barriers are those things that make it difficult for people to
connect with Christ. They will be different in every context,
but might include prejudice towards the church, a suspicion
of authority, a preoccupation with the present or a fear of
standing out from the crowd. Recognizing these barriers
enables you to identify key messages that you will need to keep
hitting if people are going to change. If fatalism is a barrier to
the gospel, then you may decide to emphasize repeatedly the
transforming power of God's Spirit.

Bridges are behaviours, beliefs, attitudes and circumstances
that offer opportunities for the gospel. An assumption that God
exists is a bridge to the gospel, even if you then need to challenge

the way people think about him. A sense of brokenness is often a bridge, as people are more willing to admit their need.

Barriers and bridges to the gospel on a south London council estate

This is how Duncan Forbes describes some of the cultural characteristics of the council estate in south London on which he grew up, and where he is now church planting. He highlights some of the barriers and bridges that exist on council estates, as well as pointing to what an indigenous church might look like.

Clothes

Clothes are a key class marker. As a kid, it was all about having the right trainers and tracksuit. You could be poor and have a trampy house, but if you had good garments to wear on the street, then you had respect. Therefore, I grew up checking out people's shoes and clothes to see if they were from the same background as me. As a child, I thought people at our church wore funny clothes. But even today, when I see white pastors dressed in a shirt and tie or wearing a blue blazer and chinos, I feel separated from them. However, I don't if they're black. Once, I walked into a church planters' consultation and saw a bloke in a smart blue suit. Immediately, I felt out of place. I felt like I didn't belong there and I felt like I wasn't a proper pastor.

Life experience and struggle

I feel my life has always been a struggle. I identify with this struggle and with other working-class people, who, I assume, have been through the same struggle. I was aware of a metanarrative of struggle in my life, but it was socially conscious hip-hop that enabled me to articulate this experience.

I know that many middle-class people have had difficult lives, but I find myself automatically assuming that they have not had as much life experience as me. When I used to share my problems with Christians, they often seemed shocked by the things that went on on our council estate and in my life, and they were clueless as to how to help me. This contributed to my feeling that the church didn't have answers to the problems that were relevant to me when I became a Christian. I had questions about how to protect my mum in an area where the police have a slow response time and seem powerless. When I asked Christians how to handle situations like this, I was usually just given a quick command to forgive and not to have vengeful thoughts. Fortunately, I was able to turn to the Bible for answers to these problems.

I wonder if the 'stiff-upper-lip' element of some middle-class preaching that does not reveal many heart issues and struggles is partly to blame for perpetuating the idea that a middle-class person doesn't know struggle. When I meet middle-class people who tell me about their suffering, such as losing a loved one, I find myself feeling more open to them and respecting them.

Respect
Having respect was one of my main goals in life. I was told to respect only those who respected me. I hardly felt any respect in middle-class churches, but I did feel this in black or American churches. One of the hardest things about being a Christian for me was losing respect and no longer being able to stand up for myself on the estate. This is something that middle-class people find hard to understand.

Models
When I was growing up, the hard nuts were my models. I remember once watching a known criminal getting chased by the police. In fact, we were all watching from the balconies of our

blocks and cheering him on. When they caught him and led him off in handcuffs, I remember thinking, 'I wanna be like him when I'm older.' When I became a Christian, there was almost no-one who could show me what a council-estate Christian man looked like. I didn't know what sanctification was supposed to look like in my life. Would there ever be a time when I would see some dodgy blokes in the street and not mentally prepare myself for a fight? Now I see part of my role as modelling what a council-estate Christian looks like.

Music

Church music never sounded anything like the music I listened to. It was either organ or guitar music. There was no urban-style music. Even the guitar music didn't sound anything like secular music. We've now made Christian hip-hop music for outreach purposes and RnB-style worship music for our church services.

God

Many people on estates in south London believe that a god (in some form) exists, but they may think that God is not interested in helping them. There is often the attitude that he has dealt them a bad set of cards, and now they have to do what they can with them.

When my mum was saved, I saw God dramatically change her. I turned to Jesus, and then we saw God miraculously provide food and money for us. However, when we went to the local Anglican church, it seemed that God wasn't alive. They advised my mum to put me up for adoption. We then went to a charismatic church, where they talked about God intervening in our life every day.

Accent

If I hear a preacher with a working-class accent, I'm on the edge of my seat thinking, 'This bloke's got something to tell me.' Even if the preaching isn't very good, I will probably still listen. However, when I hear a posh voice, my gut reaction is to think, 'He doesn't like me; he looks down on me.' Most council-estate Christians I know don't listen to British middle-class preachers online, but they do listen to US preachers like John Piper and Paul Washer.

Outspoken talk

In my culture it is acceptable (to a point) to talk in very black-and-white terms. My previous pastor once told me that I didn't respect him. I was surprised because I really did. But he found the way I talked to him uncomfortable. We've had some difficult theological discussions on our estate where the debate has gone too far, and people have been offensive. Sermons can often be more productive for us than discussions.

Moaning

Moaning and complaining is part of our culture. This can be a good opportunity to talk about why there's a struggle, and to point to God's new creation. At the same time, we are very aware that we can easily join in with the victim mentality, which is a big idol for us.

Authority

I naturally don't trust the police, the council, politicians and men in suits. But I naturally listen to my family and my friends, my own experiences of life and the Bible. As there have been pastors who have been caught stealing or womanizing, pastors cannot always be trusted.

We have overcome the distrust of authority in a number of ways. A big part of this is that we're from the estate, so we're not part of 'the system' (teachers, police, politicians and so on). My theology reflects my experiences of life, and I've placed a big emphasis on exegesis, so people know that I'm trying to find out what the Bible says. People particularly respect someone who studies the Bible for themselves, rather than just repeating what was taught at college.

Alcohol
So much of British culture is centred on alcohol, and this has caused some problems for us. I used to go into pubs to do evangelism, but then I realized that many people would assume I had backslidden if I went into a pub. In fact, some of the blokes I've discipled can't handle going into pubs, as it's too tempting. Sometimes middle-class Christians put pressure on these blokes to go out with them for a drink. However, the result is either getting drunk or withdrawing from those Christians.

Social outreach
We've done quite a lot of social action. But, over the years, as more and more agencies (secular and Christian) have done social outreach on our estate, we've seen:
- people expecting to be helped all the time
- people feeling like service-users, who are separate from the Christian service-providers
- the misunderstanding that being a Christian is about doing community work

Mapping
Another useful tool to help you understand your area is mapping. Ask a person – or preferably a small group – to draw a map of the area in which they live on a large sheet of paper, using a number of coloured marker pens. The map should not be a detailed scale representation, like a printed map. Instead, it should be impressionistic, representing those things that are important to the residents. As they draw, ask questions about

what they are drawing. Avoid leading questions like: 'Are you going to put the local school on?' The conversation is as important as the map. You are not looking for directions, but instead exploring how people perceive the place where they live, together with its strengths and weaknesses.

If you get the opportunity, repeat the exercise with a second person or group. With larger groups, you could divide them into two or more groups and ask them to draw their maps at the same time. Compare the two maps and the two conversations. What local features were important? What issues about the local community and its needs did the exercise raise? How did the perceptions and priorities of the two people or groups differ? With larger groups, did this exercise generate any discussion? What were the disagreements?

Transect walking
'A good place to start,' according to Dai Hankey in South Wales, 'is to walk the streets with your eyes open.' 'Jesus didn't walk this world with his head in a holy shekinah cloud, but with his eyes peeled for opportunities to demonstrate and proclaim the gospel.'[14]

- Jesus saw disciples in sinners: 'After this [Jesus] went out and saw a tax collector named Levi, sitting at the tax booth. And he said to him, "Follow me"' (Luke 5:27 ESV).
- Jesus looked with compassion on the masses: 'When he drew near and saw the city, he wept over it' (Luke 19:41 ESV).
- Jesus looked with compassion on individuals: 'When Jesus saw her weeping, and the Jews who had come with her also weeping, he was deeply moved in his spirit and greatly troubled' (John 11:33 ESV).

- Jesus saw faith and responded to it: 'When Jesus saw their faith, he said to the paralytic, "Take heart, my son; your sins are forgiven"' (Matthew 9:2 ESV).
- Jesus saw need and met it: 'When Jesus entered Peter's house, he saw his mother-in-law lying sick with a fever. He touched her hand, and the fever left her, and she rose and began to serve him' (Matthew 8:14–15 ESV).

Community development practitioners talk about 'transect walking' – walking through an area in order to analyse a cross section or a 'slice' of the neighbourhood. As you walk, identify different residential and commercial zones, private and public spaces, ethnic and social groups. Look at how people care for their homes, how they dress, how they interact. Track the movement of people: Where are they going? Where do they congregate? What communal activities take place in the area? What opportunities are there to connect with or serve the community?

Take a local person with you and ask them to explain what is happening. They will be able to show you how different areas are viewed, the haunts of various groups, problem issues and crime spots, how the local economy works, and so on. Encourage them to use what you see together as prompts to tell you stories from the community's history.

Walking the streets with your eyes open[15]
Dai Hankey shares the following stories from his experience of planting Hill City Church in South Wales.

1. Playground
For over a year before we had even moved to the estate, my wife and I committed to prayer-walking the streets every Monday

---

evening, whatever the weather. We did this with our spiritual eyes open. One evening we stumbled across a derelict playground that lay right at the centre of the estate. It had clearly been abandoned for years and served no purpose, apart from giving residents somewhere to dump rubbish. All that remained of the playground were two rusty metal benches that had been shoved so far into the ground that, to sit on them, meant sitting at ground level. However, we did just that, and as we gazed at shards of broken glass, the unwanted junk and the general desolation that surrounded us, we were led (by the Spirit) to pray that God would establish a place of worship here at the heart of the estate. After we'd prayed, we looked over our shoulders and saw a house for sale. To cut a long story short, several months later we bought that house, moved in and did exactly what we'd prayed about – we started a church in that house and established a place of worship there! The opportunities we've had to share the gospel purely by living in this part of the community are way too numerous (and sensitive) to write about here, but, suffice to say, it was a God thing!

Furthermore, upon moving in, we made it our aim as a fledgling church to see the ruins rebuilt and this derelict playground restored, so that the local kids could have somewhere to play again. We believe firmly that Christians in broken communities should have a reputation as 'the restorer of streets to dwell in' (Isaiah 58:12 ESV). So we prayed, got in touch with the council and started the ball rolling on a three-year £250,000 process that eventually led to the total restoration of the play area. Hill City Church was right at the heart of the project from the start, even sponsoring the mural on the wall. Our involvement has certainly opened doors for the gospel. However, *none* of this would have happened if we hadn't walked the streets with our eyes open all those years ago.

2. Rubbish

Another occasion when open eyes have led to opportunities to demonstrate the gospel came in the area of rubbish. I'm not exaggerating when I say that the fly-tipping and dumping of litter around where we live was one of the most dangerous and disgusting issues that we faced when we moved here. Coupled with the local youths' habit of robbing wheelie-bins, surfing down the road on them, and then burning them out at the bottom, this had led to trash carnage. Sometimes my kids had to wade through used nappies just to get to the car. That really wound me up.

That was until I opened my eyes. Literally, one day God revealed to me that I should take responsibility for this rubbish. All of it! I was confronted with the perfect opportunity to demonstrate grace. So I started making phone calls and getting the council to sort things out. But I also went out myself with a litter picker and gloves, collecting it all up and putting it in my own bin. Why? Because, the more I thought about it, the more I saw this as a perfect platform to illustrate what Christ had done for us on the cross. He stepped into our mess, taking away our filth, for free, never to let it be seen again!

3. Assault

One of our most harrowing experiences took place on Christmas Day a few years ago. I was still awake at around 1am when I heard a noise outside. I looked out of my window to see a woman getting beaten senseless by a man, right outside my house. I ran out to intervene. By the time I got out there, he was kicking her in the face and stamping on her head. I shouted at him and he ran off. The woman got up, swore at me and ran after him!

So was it a waste of my time to get involved? No. Firstly, because it was the right thing to do. Secondly, because, over the days that followed, it became clear that there had been several other men who had witnessed the assault from their windows, yet had chosen to do nothing. The fact that I was the only neighbour to step in seemed to speak volumes about who I worship. I didn't do it to be a hero. I did it because it wasn't an option to turn a blind eye. But having open eyes can sometimes break your heart.

4. Graffiti
A gang of around twenty youths had decided to make the bus stop in front of my mate Jim's house their new haunt. This involved drinking, noise, setting things on fire and relieving themselves in the street. I knew that Jim was praying about the situation, but it still bothered him.

As I left his house one morning, I saw a huge list of names scrawled all over his bus stop. And that's when God opened my eyes. 'Jim!' I shouted. 'You've got a whole list of names to pray for here. You've got your own prayer-list.' It might sound stupid, but I've never walked past graffiti in the same way since. All around us in these estates are lists of names that represent real young people who are lost, broken and crying out for attention.

Start walking your streets with your eyes open. Who knows what God will show you?

Loving people in working-class and deprived areas

Love is the New Testament's core missiological principle.

You don't need a social science degree to work in urban contexts. You don't need a theory of contextualization. You need love. Love is the New Testament's core missiological principle.

Love is thoughtful. It thinks about the other person. It considers their needs. It communicates in their language. Love listens to people. It is interested in their hopes and hurts. Love does not treat people in an undifferentiated, generic way or according to some theory of contextualization. It recognizes that each person is different. Andy Mason says,

> I reflect a lot on cultural differences, but I don't talk about this much in my church because I don't want to highlight those differences. The gospel should generate self-forgetfulness. The thing that generates racism is a focus on my own culture and its distinctives. Where the focus is on Jesus, then relationships between believers of different cultures will happen naturally.

This does not mean that we have to find people lovable. Sometimes people will enrich our lives. Sometimes they will be a pain in the neck. And this is true of people from all social classes. But we must love them, whether they are lovable or not, *because of Jesus*. He is our model, loving the unlovable, giving his life for his enemies:

> God has poured out his love into our hearts by the Holy Spirit, whom he has given us. You see, at just the right time, when we were still powerless, Christ died for the ungodly. Very rarely will anyone die for a righteous man, though for a good man someone might possibly dare to die. But God demonstrates his own love for us in this: While we were still sinners, Christ died for us.
>
> (Romans 5:5–8)

3 KEY GOSPEL THEMES FOR WORKING-CLASS AND DEPRIVED AREAS

We don't have a different gospel for working-class and deprived areas. The unchanging gospel speaks to all of life, is richly textured and can be presented in myriad forms. However, we want to teach it in all its fullness. We also recognize that there can be different starting points, and the most appropriate starting points will vary from situation to situation.

We also need to recognize that some cultures have particular barriers that need to be addressed in the course of gospel proclamation. Tim Keller speaks of 'defeater beliefs' – assumptions that trump everything else. However persuasive you may be, a person will not respond to your message until their defeater beliefs are addressed. There aren't many atheists on housing estates. 'People have a supernaturalist worldview,' says Mez McConnell. 'Over 90% of the women in the church toddler groups have visited a spiritist or medium. It's embarrassing how easy it is to talk about Jesus.' But people do have defeater beliefs that prevent them from putting their faith in Christ. Steve Casey from Speke Baptist Church in Liverpool says, 'Theologically, I expect the marginalized, underprivileged and outsiders to be more receptive to the gospel. Yet there seems to be an ingrained suspicion of church, and an assumed understanding of the message that leads many in our community to reject Christ before they have even heard it.'

So we're going to identify some key gospel themes with which it is helpful to lead, or upon which it is important to touch. These are significant truths for any congregation, but experience suggests that they resonate especially with those from deprived backgrounds. (As with the cultural characteristics identified in the previous chapter, these are generally true for working-class and deprived areas, but you may want to identify the specific themes that are most relevant in your context.) We will start with a list, before exploring three in more depth.

Key gospel themes

The fatherhood of God
Many of the urban poor will have had difficult or non-existent relationships with their fathers. This will often affect their view of God, so it is important to show how God is a loving Father who invites us to be his children.

The family of God
The gospel also invites us into the family of the church. Adoption into the family can be particularly poignant if you don't have a mother or father or a functional relationship with your parents.

The sovereignty of God

This is a liberating and comforting truth for people whose everyday life is marked by struggle. Trusting in God's sovereignty allows us to trust that God can bring good out of bad situations. Trusting in God as judge also allows us to refrain from taking justice into our own hands.

The lordship of God

One church planter says, 'In the black community [in London], everyone thinks they're cool with God. Their understanding of God is distorted by experience, church exposure and theology, what has been handed down or picked up from TV. Just believing that God is there is good enough. Therefore, we have had to place a strong emphasis on sin, sinfulness and true lordship. We need to stress the pre-eminence of God, as otherwise he is compartmentalized.'

The grace of God

Most people from working-class and deprived areas start with an assumption that Christianity is about being good or being religious. If you call them to follow Christ, then they will hear this as a call to live a good life. So we need to be constantly subverting these false ideas by showing how the gospel contrasts with legalism.

People on housing estates are less hung up on traditional church practices than many Christians, says Mez McConnell. They expect a church to be a church, with prayers, hymns and sermons. Indeed, people often still trust in historic church buildings. 'It's often said, "It's easier to give birth than to raise the dead" – but not in housing schemes. The established church still has capital.' Small groups meeting elsewhere are viewed as cults. People don't meet up in a house, except to do drugs. Small groups work for established Christians, but not for mission. Niddrie Community Church has four annual events for unbelievers: a Christmas service, an Easter fry-up, an *X Factor* night and Niddrie's Got Talent. Lots of people come to the Easter fry-up, but they wouldn't come if it were held the following week, without the Easter connection.

So the problem is not that the church needs to be more contemporary or gimmicky. The problem is that people think they are not good enough for church. 'They're scared of church,' says Mez, 'more than you're scared of them.'

The justice of God

In a culture where there can be a lot of violence and hurt, there is a strong temptation to seek revenge. In this context, it is important to teach people to rest in God's sovereignty and leave room for *God's* wrath. We do not need to take revenge, because God will ensure justice is done for the wrongs perpetrated against us – either at the cross if the wrong-doer becomes a Christian, or on the day of judgment. It is also important to teach individuals about justification. They too are perpetrators of wrong who need to be justified before God through the cross. Sometimes people are wary of teaching this technical aspect of salvation, but experience suggests that it is actually readily understood, and often more deeply appreciated, in a culture where court appearances are common.

It can also be important to speak of the social dimensions of God's justice. In the twentieth century, the emphasis on social justice in liberal theology often made it suspect among evangelicals who feared that a concern for social issues might eclipse personal evangelism.[1] As a result, says Martyn Lloyd-Jones,

The impression has gained currency that to be a Christian, and more especially an evangelical, means that we are traditionalists, and advocates of the status quo. I believe that this largely accounts for our failure in this country to make contact with the so-called working-classes . . . Far too often, as Nonconformist men have got on in the world, and made money and become Managers and Owners, they have become opponents of the working-classes who were agitating for their rights.[2]

Rachel was a single mother who was converted in our church. She lived under the threat of domestic violence. She told my wife that, at first, she was not really sure if she fitted into our church. But she kept coming back because, in our teaching, we applied the Bible to social injustices. She heard the Bible speaking into her situation.

The new creation

As we have seen, the urban poor often see their lives as a story of struggle and hopelessness. We can associate this with the brokenness of a world marred by sin, and point to God's coming new world when 'the struggle' will be over. Wayne Gordon says, 'If the Christ of the suburbs is the Christ of forgiveness, the Christ of the city is the Christ of hope. Ultimately, of course, Jesus offers both, but recognising differences in perceived needs plays an important role in forming strategies for evangelism.'[3]

Eschatological speculation is a popular topic among black youths who are exposed to all sorts of speculation about what's going to happen in the end days. We can take advantage of this enthusiasm to clarify what will happen when Jesus returns.

The purpose of life

Many residents on council estates feel their life has no purpose. They lack the motivation to do more than watch TV or play

computer games. We can present the good news that they were
made for a better life. Christ has better things for us than being
drugged by a screen. This is a good context in which to teach
about God's mission, spiritual gifts and the body of Christ.

The freedom to change

It is common in deprived areas to believe you cannot change.
The circumstances of people's lives, as we've already seen, have
left them with low aspirations. So it is important to emphasize
that we really can change, with God's help, and we can begin
to win battles with sin. This truth can readily be reinforced
through testimonies of change.

The futility of self-righteousness

People on council estates are not immune to self-righteousness.
'I'm a moral burglar, for I only rob people who can afford it. I
don't steal from handicapped and elderly. People who do that
are scumbags.' 'I'm an alcoholic, but I'm not a druggie.' 'I'm a
druggie, but I'm not an alcoholic.' Self-righteousness takes
many forms. Paul Watt, Senior Lecturer in Urban Studies at
Birkbeck University in London, writes,

> 'Respectability' proved to be an important lens through which
> many tenants assessed themselves, their neighbours and their
> neighbourhoods. They made strenuous efforts to distantiate
> themselves [keep themselves at a distance] from the 'rough' elements
> around them and in so doing maintain their own respectability in
> straitened circumstances. They emphasized the distinction between
> those ordinary, decent council-house dwellers like themselves, and
> those low-status others who in one way or another were 'rough' and
> caused 'problems'.[4]

* * *

Having identified a number of key gospel themes, let's now explore three in more depth. Our aim is not to say all that could be said about these themes, but to highlight how, specifically, they offer good news to people from working-class or deprived areas.

The remainder of this chapter is based on material from Duncan Forbes, a church planter on a council estate in south London. These truths are not proclaimed by an outsider, but from the personal experience of growing up on a council estate.

The fatherhood of God

We have all had different experiences of fathers, and these can shape our view of God. If your dad was not good, it is possible that, when you think of God the Father, you may, perhaps only subconsciously, view God the way you viewed your dad. If your dad never listened to you, then you may think that God doesn't listen to you. If your dad never protected you, then you may think God will not keep you safe. If your dad was never around for you, then you may think God will not be there for you. If we judge God by our experience of fatherhood, we can miss out on the wonderful experience of knowing God as our Father.

God the Father has an eternal relationship of perfect love with God the Son. Wonderfully, Jesus came to earth so that we can come into this relationship. So everyone who puts their faith in Jesus Christ comes into this perfect relationship. If you've put your faith in Christ, then you are adopted by God the Father. God the Father loves you with the same perfect love that he has for his Son, Jesus.

God is a father who seeks us out. Maybe you feel your dad ignored you. Maybe he was out at work all the time or engrossed in TV. But God the Father seeks people out. In Ezekiel, God says,

'I myself will search for my sheep and look after them' (Ezekiel 34:11).

God is a father who welcomes us. Maybe you feel your dad never really accepted you or was rarely pleased with you. But God the Father's great forgiveness and welcome are seen in the parable of the prodigal son (Luke 15). Maybe your dad was stern and harsh with you. God sent his Son to take the judgment we deserve on the cross. In Christ, God accepts us and delights in us.

God is a father who cares for us. Maybe you feel like your dad abandoned you. Psalm 27:10 (ESV) says,

> For my father and my mother have forsaken me,
>   but the LORD will take me in.

God doesn't turn away anyone who comes to him. Maybe your dad didn't provide for you, but Jesus says our heavenly Father gives us good gifts (Luke 11:11–13).

God is a father who treasures us. Maybe you feel like your dad was disappointed in you, that you were never special to him. God calls his people his 'treasured possession' (Exodus 19:4–6).

God is a father who loves us. Maybe you feel like your dad never really loved you. 'How great is the love the Father has lavished on us, that we should be called children of God! And that is what we are!' (1 John 3:1). How much does God love us? 'For God so loved the world that he gave his one and only Son' (John 3:16).

God is 'a father to the fatherless' (Psalm 68:5). If you never knew your dad, or he wasn't around much or wasn't good to you, then you may feel like you were fatherless. But if you turn to God, then he will adopt you and make up for your absent or bad dad. Your Father God will never fail you (Psalm 32:10) or lie to you (Hebrews 6:18). He'll always show compassion to you (2 Corinthians 1:3). He heals our hurts (Psalm 34:18) and turns our sadness into gladness (Lamentations 3:32–33). He's happy with us when we do what is right (Proverbs 23:15–16; 27:11; 1 John 4:10) and forgives us when we do what is wrong (Luke 15).

God is also a father who disciplines (Hebrews 12:5–12). We usually want to run away from discipline, but it is in fact a good thing. A loving father disciplines and trains his children. And God our Father is no different. He trains us through the Bible and the words of other Christians (Proverbs 3:1). He also trains us through suffering. Life's problems are not a sign that God is angry with us, rather a sign that God loves us 'because the Lord disciplines those he loves, and he punishes everyone he accepts as a son' (Hebrews 12:6). I don't give my children everything they want or remove all pain from their lives, because I don't want them to be spoiled brats. Suffering is all part of being a son or daughter.

'We have all had human fathers who disciplined us and we respected them for it. How much more should we submit to the Father of our spirits and live!' (Hebrews 12:9). You might find this a hard verse, because you've not received any discipline from your dad, or not in a way you respected. But the point is that, if you endured your dad's discipline, how much more you should endure God's discipline, which is always wise and always loving. The result of God's discipline in those who accept it is holiness, righteousness and peace (Hebrews 12:10–11).

Victim mentality

Victim mentality is not so much a gospel theme as a key issue, as we have seen, for those living in deprived areas, and it is addressed by the gospel in a number of ways.

But, in fact, victim mentality is also common elsewhere. It has been part of fallen humanity from the beginning of time.

The 'victim', when Adam and Eve ate the fruit in the Garden of Eden in Genesis 3, was God. But Adam blamed God for giving him Eve, and Eve blamed the serpent. They portrayed themselves as victims of God and of Satan. And we continue to pass the blame today: 'I did it because I was treated badly'; 'I've had a hard life, so that's why I'm the way I am'; 'I did it because I felt so lonely.'

Seeing ourselves as victims allows us to justify our actions. We view ourselves as special cases. When Saul offers sacrifices without waiting for Samuel in 1 Samuel 13, he makes excuses. He sees his sinful actions as justified. Today, people may say they commit crime because they grew up on a council estate. But not everyone from an estate commits crime, and many crimes are committed by people not from estates. When we think we're victims, we give ourselves permission to sin.

I read about Saul, and I think about the guys I meet on the street who are totally paranoid. Having a victim mentality is a bit like wearing tinted glasses. We begin to see every comment through these lenses and interpret them as a threat. David is loyal to Saul and refuses to do anything to harm him, even when the opportunity is presented to him. Yet Saul sees him as a threat and keeps trying to kill him. We too can see people as enemies who are not really enemies at all.

A victim mentality can cause us to resent God's compassion for other people. Jonah doesn't want to go to Nineveh, because he suspects God might have mercy on the Ninevites, Israel's enemies. And Jonah sulks when God does indeed show mercy. In a similar way, when some of us see a policeman, we think, 'He's going to stop and search me.' So we wear the tinted glasses and start to feel we're the good ones who deserve God's compassion, while the police are terrible people. We like to hear bad stories about them. When we see a police officer, the last thing on our mind is sharing God's compassion with them. In the belly of the fish, Jonah recognizes that 'those who cling to worthless idols forfeit the mercy that could be theirs'. Jonah is not just talking about pagan people. He himself needs to turn in repentance from the idol of a victim mentality and look instead to the Lord for salvation (Jonah 2:8–9).

'Look after number one'; 'I wouldn't take that if I were you'; 'Make sure people treat you with respect.' These are the ways people fight back when they feel threatened. But in 2 Corinthians 10:3–4, Paul says, 'Though we live in the world, we do not wage war as the world does. The weapons we fight with are not the weapons of the world.' The weapons of a victim mentality do not work. People often respond to mistreatment by becoming hard. They think they are protecting themselves, but really they are making themselves bitter and cutting themselves off from true relationships.

In 2 Corinthians 10:4–5 Paul continues, 'On the contrary, they have divine power to demolish strongholds. We demolish arguments and every pretension that sets itself up against the knowledge of God, and we take captive every thought to make it obedient to Christ.' So what is there in this 'knowledge of God' that equips us to destroy the arguments of a victim mentality?

The sovereignty of God

What if I really am a victim? How can I recognize this and still avoid a victim *mentality*? Joseph was sold into slavery by his brothers, falsely accused of attempted rape and thrown into prison. He was let down by the chief cupbearer whom he had helped. How did he react? He could have been bitter, or been paranoid like Saul. He could have tried to control people. Instead, he did good, and his actions led to the saving of many lives.

How did he do this? When he reveals himself to his brothers, he says, 'Do not be distressed and do not be angry with yourselves for selling me here, because it was to save lives that God sent me ahead of you' (Genesis 45:5). Joseph views his hardships in the light of God's sovereignty, recognizing that God is in control of everything that happens in his life. He says that 'God sent [him]' to Egypt. He knows that his brothers did this to him, but he recognizes God's sovereignty in that very act. 'We know that in all things God works for the good of those who love him' (Romans 8:28). Joseph didn't necessarily understand everything God had done in his life, but he was content to trust that God was a good God. We too can say, 'I might not be able to know what God is doing right now, but I do know that he is good.'

Here is one of the best ways to avoid victim mentality: recognize God's sovereignty in your life. He is the one who has put you in that situation, and he has a purpose for it. It could lead to the salvation of other people. You might discover the depths of God's love in the midst of hardship. You might be able to pass on the comfort you have received in your hardship.

The justice of God

Avoiding a victim mentality does not mean that we have to pretend we are never victims. We still recognize that God is grieved over the sins that other people do to us. There will still be judgment, and God is the judge. God's judgment was poured out on Jesus on the cross, or it will be poured out at the end of time.

Jesus is our supreme example (1 Peter 2:21–25). He was the ultimate victim of injustice. He suffered, even though he had done nothing wrong. He was betrayed by a friend, unjustly tried, beaten, mocked and finally nailed to a cross to die alone. But he didn't respond in a sinful way. Instead, he entrusted himself to God.

The mission of God

In 2 Timothy 2, Paul says that Christians are like soldiers. Soldiers don't expect comfort. They expect hardship and war. We are to accept our share of suffering as good soldiers of Christ. Our mission is to pass on the gospel. Paul was beaten, shipwrecked, imprisoned, threatened. He could easily have felt sorry for himself and viewed himself as a victim. But his main concern was passing on the gospel. This put his hardship into perspective. He called on Timothy to embrace suffering for the sake of the gospel in the same way. Next time things don't go your way or someone treats you badly, stop and think, 'How could I share the gospel in this situation? How can I be a good soldier of Christ in this situation?'

I recently found myself in a situation where people blanked me. At first I was angry. I thought they had dissed me because I was from a council estate. But then, I realized it was just a cultural difference, and I was simply interpreting the situation through my victim mentality. So I'm left asking myself, 'Why does it bother me so much?' The answer is that I think I'm important, and I'm upset when other people don't know how important I am. But does the Bible say that people should acknowledge me? No, it says I'm a terrible sinner. So I realize I'm guilty of self-love and self-importance. I forget that Jesus is more wonderful and more important than I am. I'm setting myself up as king in my kingdom. I've learned to repent, asking God to forgive me and give me the grace to change. This is how I can demolish my pretension, take my victim mentality captive and make it obedient to Christ.

The sovereignty of God[5]

Living on a council estate does my head in. It's hard to cope. It's not where I want to live. The doctrine that most helps me to live where I do is the sovereignty of God.

Here is a council-estate view of God, albeit a generalization:

> God does exist, but he's not in control of everything. God has dealt me a set of cards, and now it's my job to do the best I can with them. I'm going to take care of number one and my family, because no-one else is going to care for me. Life is a big struggle. We're trying to take care of ourselves. But this is tough. We commit sins along the way. We need to protect ourselves, so we have a vicious dog or carry a knife. We feel like victims. We spend our lives being aggressive towards injustice. 'Are you going to take that?' we ask each other. It sometimes leads to vigilante attacks, because no-one else is going to establish justice. So we set ourselves up as God. We want to be the person in control. We want to be the provider, the judge, the avenger, the enforcer.

But the Bible teaches that God is in control. He is the Provider, the Judge, the Avenger, the Enforcer. So we need to correct people's view of God.

Here are some aspects of the sovereignty of God that are important to proclaim in deprived areas.

1. God is in charge

> The LORD sits enthroned over the flood;
>> the LORD is enthroned as King for ever.
> (Psalm 29:10)

The pagan religions believed the gods fought for control, with the sea as the battleground and chaos as the result. But this psalm asserts that Yahweh is the one in charge. On estates it can feel like different forces are battling for control, and the result is chaos. Some people think the youth on their estate are in charge, so they are afraid. Or the council or the police are in charge, and this can make them feel unsettled.

But 'the LORD is enthroned over the flood.' Your estate is run by God. This psalm recalls God's sovereignty in bringing order out of primordial chaos in Genesis 1, and through the renewal after the flood in Genesis 6 – 9 and the redemption through the sea in Exodus 14. In Revelation 21, at the end of the Bible, there is no more sea. Chaos is defeated. Sometimes you go off the estate and have a good time. When you return, you have a sinking feeling. We need a constant reminder that God is in charge of our council estates.

2. God is in control of both good and bad things

We often think that God is in charge of the good things. But God is also in charge when bad things happen:

> Who can speak and have it happen
>   if the Lord has not decreed it?
> Is it not from the mouth of the Most High
>   that both calamities and good things come?
> (Lamentations 3:37–38)

It is not only that God *permits* evil. 'I form the light and create darkness, I bring prosperity and create disaster; I, the LORD, do all these things' (Isaiah 45:7). The Lord *creates* 'disaster'.

On a council estate, there is drama going on all over the place. People live for drama. It can feel like we live in a soap-opera script. People need to know that God is in control of the script. He is in control of the calamity in their lives – the financial calamities, the crime we experience, and so on.

To this day, my teeth hurt from a time when I was attacked by a gang. But I find it comforting to know that Jesus holds everything together, including those perpetrators, even as they punched me. And he is infinitely wise. God is not evil. But he does create the disasters in our lives, and why does he do this? What do we say to people facing calamity?

People need to know that God is in control of the script.

1. It is better that God creates the disasters than that someone else does. You don't want Satan creating disaster in your life, because he doesn't like you. You don't want other people doing it, because they'll put themselves first. You don't want to be creating your own disasters, because no-one is big enough to control those disasters – there will always be a situation that you cannot handle. It is God who brings chaos, and this is good news because he is able to control the chaos.

2. God creates disasters to make us more like Christ: 'We know that in all things God works for the good of those who love him, who have been called according to his purpose. For those God foreknew he also predestined to be conformed to the likeness of his Son, that he might be the firstborn among many brothers' (Romans 8:28–29). People often say that quoting this in times of crisis is callous, but please do quote this to me because I need to hear it! The good things and the bad things – including the things that have caused me deep emotional turmoil – all are there to make me like Jesus.

This helps counter the response of victim mode. If, early on, I recognize that God has brought something into my life to make me like Jesus, I can avoid a victim mentality. And becoming like Jesus is more valuable than avoiding the disaster.

Suddenly the soap-opera script of my life has meaning.

3. It is good that God creates disaster, because it helps us to forgive people. Human beings are responsible for their actions, and it is important to teach this, as otherwise people abdicate responsibility. But God uses sinful actions – including the sinful actions done against us – for good.

'Joseph said [to the brothers who had sold him into slavery], "Don't be afraid. Am I in the place of God? You intended to harm me, but God intended it for good to accomplish what is now being done, the saving of many lives. So then, don't be afraid. I will provide for you and your children." And he reassured them and spoke kindly to them' (Genesis 50:19–21). Many people on council estates would not respond in the way Joseph does. Even if we did forgive people, we would not reassure them with kindness, as Joseph does. Joseph avoided a victim mentality through his understanding of the sovereignty of God. Because he saw God's purpose in his brothers' cruelty, he could forgive them.

Many of us on council estates have a chip on our shoulders. We can become bitter and unforgiving. But, if we can understand that God caused our calamity and he is using it to make us like Jesus, then we will not be bitter or unforgiving.

3. God is in control of our physical safety

In our area, children plan their route to school to avoid getting attacked. I've heard teenagers say they can't go to college next day because a gang has threatened to beat them up. Elderly people do not leave their houses, for fear of getting robbed. Physical protection is a big issue.

Here is a prayer to pray before you leave the house or in any situation when you feel threatened: 'I do not need to carry a blade or get a vicious dog, because I've got my minder – the Lord.' And if we do get hurt, this is something that God has created to make us like Christ, because being like Christ is more valuable than not getting hurt. This also means I can avoid taking vengeance.

> O Lord my God, I take refuge in you;
>   save and deliver me from all who pursue me,
> or they will tear me like a lion
>   and rip me to pieces with no-one to rescue me.
> (Psalm 7:1–2)

4. God has sovereignly arranged deprived neighbourhoods for our benefit

Everything and everyone has told me I need to escape from my council estate. But if I believe that God determined my council estate and my place in it, so that I would search for him, then that will change my attitude. It will mean that I cannot complain about my upbringing. God arranged that I would be a scared kid living high up in a tower block with a sick mother, so that I would find him. If I had grown up somewhere else, then I might not be a Christian now.

> From one man he made every nation of men, that they should inhabit the whole earth; and he determined the times set for them and the exact places where they should live. God did this so that men would seek him and perhaps reach out for him and find him, though he is not far from each one of us.
> (Acts 17:26–27)

God arranged my deprived neighbourhood for my benefit. And God continues to determine my council estate as his means of sanctification in my life (Romans 8:28–29).

It is important that we proclaim this, because many people cannot stand living on their estate. Many of us have seen ministries grow, only to see them die back, because people have moved on. It is not always wrong to leave an estate, but we must not see the estate as an enemy to be avoided. Everything changes if we view our council estate as God's means to save us and make us like Jesus.

5. Nothing can stop God accomplishing his purpose

In deprived areas, many of us feel powerless. We believe that power belongs to politicians or bankers. This is why many of us do not pursue middle-class means of improvement. It took years for the council to mend a broken window in our flat when I was a child. So I grew up assuming that the authorities were not there to help. I remember a middle-class friend phoning the police after an incident with his son. I assumed nothing would happen. But, almost immediately, he had an interview with a high-ranking officer. I remember a well-known Christian speaker saying, 'I know what it's like to plant a small church – on my first week I only had eighty people.' This kind of statement crushes you, when your church has been ten to twenty people for years.

And so we feel powerless. We feel like we don't have the resources to plant a church. Is God going to help people with their addictions? Is God going to save people involved in crime? Is God really going to help us plant a church?

I make known the end from the beginning,
     from ancient times, what is still to come.
I say: My purpose will stand,
     and I will do all that I please.
(Isaiah 46:10)

I know that you can do all things;
     no plan of yours can be thwarted.
(Job 42:2)

Nothing can stop God accomplishing his purpose. Jesus promised to build his church. So we can drop our excuses and our victim mentality.

6. God is in control of who gets saved
Salvation does not 'depend on man's desire or effort, but on God's mercy'.

> For [God] says to Moses,
>
> > 'I will have mercy on whom I have mercy,
> >   and I will have compassion on whom I have compassion.'
> (Romans 9:15–16)

> The Lord's servant must not quarrel; instead, he must be kind to everyone, able to teach, not resentful. Those who oppose him he must gently instruct, in the hope that God will grant them repentance leading them to a knowledge of the truth, and that they will come to their senses and escape from the trap of the devil, who has taken them captive to do his will.
> (2 Timothy 2:24–26)

If God wants to give repentance, then he will. Why is this important? In most deprived areas, people are not queuing up to come to church. It can be discouraging. It is important to remember that God is in control of who gets saved. Someone in our church said, 'Shane is a guy who can't be saved.' But, within a year, God in his sovereignty had saved him. Shane got saved as a Calvinist, because God's sovereignty was so clear in his experience!

This stops us becoming proud. As Christians, we lose our rough edges and can all too easily start thinking we are better than other people. But remembering that we are who we are, only because God chose us, will stop us becoming proud. 'The only reason I'm not beating my wife is because God chose me'; 'The only reason I'm not off my head on drugs is because God chose me.'

The truth that God is sovereign is not new. But when we make the links to people's everyday experience, the sovereignty of God becomes good news for people in deprived areas.

4 EVANGELISM IN WORKING-CLASS AND DEPRIVED AREAS

Suppose you meet someone who is depressed because he is unemployed. What do you do? Here are some options.

1. You could tell him the gospel. You could tell him that he was made to know God, but his sin separates him from God. God sent Jesus to die in his place, to take the judgment he deserves, so he can be right with God.

With this approach, the priority is evangelism, and evangelism is understood as the logical presentation of certain core gospel truths.

2. You could help him find a job. You could assist him with his CV, interview skills and motivation. You could search local job centres, papers and websites with him for vacancies. You could even start a small enterprise, to provide employment for him and others like him. He knows you are a Christian, so you

hope he will make the connection between your actions and Jesus.

With this approach, the priority is social involvement. The problem is that, if he does make any connections, he will interpret your actions through a legalistic framework, assuming that you are doing good to make yourself right with God, and that, if he is to know God, then he must become respectable and kind like you.

3. You could do both 1 and 2. You could help him find a job, hoping that a gospel opportunity opens up. You may hope he will ask at some point, 'Why are you doing this?' You are then ready to respond, 'Because of the love of Jesus'.

With this approach, social involvement and evangelism are side by side, but not intersecting. This is where most evangelicals are.

4. You could use the presenting issue as a window into the heart, so that you contextualize the gospel on a person-by-person basis. In the above example, you might gently ask, 'Why does not having a job make you depressed?' This would create a conversation about identity and meaning, or a conversation about proving yourself, which might in time lead on to a conversation about self-justification and justification by faith.

Options 1 and 3 present the gospel, but in a way that does not connect with people's lives. Option 2 connects with people's lives, but neglects the true and lasting hope of the gospel. By focusing on the desires or idolatries of the heart, we can begin to connect the gospel to people's lives.

Enter, explore, expose, evangelize

Dan Strange of Oak Hill College, London, suggests a fourfold approach to mission in any culture: enter, explore, expose, evangelize. There is perhaps a fifth 'e' that precedes these stages, which is 'engage'. We are to engage with people in the ways suggested in the previous chapter, and we are to engage with God in prayer.

At the heart of this approach is the recognition that the alternative to the worship of God is the worship of idols. We need to engage with the idolatries of the community and individuals we are trying to reach. One advantage of this approach is its holistic nature. Our evangelism can be merely intellectual or reason-led. But talking about idolatry does not just deal with what I *think* about the world, but also what I *feel* and *desire*. God says,

> My people have committed two sins:
> They have forsaken me,
>   the spring of living water,
> and have dug their own cisterns,
>   broken cisterns that cannot hold water.
> (Jeremiah 2:13)

People have turned away from the fountain of living water and are trying to lick water from muddy holes in the ground. Our job as evangelists is to show people the paucity of their cisterns and how they can get the true, living water they desire.

Enter

Ted Turnau talks about a worldview tree. The *roots* of the tree are the ultimate *commitments* of a person's worldview. The *trunk* is the *story*, out of which people construct their lives, the story they tell to explain life. The *branches* are the *answers* they therefore provide to the big metaphysical and ethical questions of life. These include the way they perceive themselves, their source of authority and their basis for determining right and wrong. The *fruit* is the *culture* we produce: the behavioural norms, jokes, sayings, art and so on which reflect our underlying commitments and narrative. A person's worldview is made up of all of these elements.

Explore

The 'explore' stage of the process involves assessing a community's worldview against the Bible's worldview. In particular, we are looking for idolatries. What are the commitments, beliefs, longings and desires that we substitute for a relationship with the living God?

But we are also looking for signs of common grace. Idols are parasites, distortions of what is good. They are desires for what is good that have become misdirected. A desire for belonging, for example, that should lead us into relationship with God instead becomes a controlling desire for sexual partners or membership of gang culture.

Expose

In the context of exposing the folly of making a god from a piece of wood, Isaiah says,

> They know nothing, they understand nothing;
>> their eyes are plastered over so that they cannot see,
>> and their minds closed so that they cannot understand.
> No-one stops to think,
>> no-one has the knowledge or understanding to say,
> 'Half of it I used for fuel;
>> I even baked bread over its coals,
>> I roasted meat and I ate.
> Shall I make a detestable thing from what is left?
>> Shall I bow down to a block of wood?'
> He feeds on ashes, a deluded heart misleads him;

> he cannot save himself, or say,
>
>   'Is not this thing in my right hand a lie?'
>
> (Isaiah 44:18–20)

'No-one stops to think.' Our role is to make people stop and think. We need to expose, as Isaiah does, the folly of idolatry. Idols do not, cannot deliver. And, if we stop and think, we can see the folly of finding identity or fulfilment in other human beings or inanimate objects. Intellectual approaches show that unbelief does not work at an intellectual level. The idolatry approach shows that unbelief does not work at any level!

Evangelize

As we expose the idolatry of people's hearts, we can also point them to the fountain of life in the cross of Jesus. In the language of Jeremiah 2, we both expose the brokenness of their cisterns *and* point them to 'the spring of living water'. The gospel is both an appeal and appealing. In other words, it fulfils the hopes in the culture, but in a way that challenges the assumptions of the culture. It offers what missiologist Hendrik Kraemer calls a 'subversive fulfilment'.[1] It is subversive because it includes a challenge to repent of our idolatry and believe the truth about God. It is a fulfilment because it offers the fulfilment of the underlying hopes and desires within the culture. This is what Paul is saying in 1 Corinthians 1, when he speaks of the cross as the power and wisdom of God. The Jews want power, and the Greeks want wisdom. And the cross is true power and true wisdom, but not in the way people expected. It both fulfils and subverts those cultures' longing for power and wisdom.

There are some evangelical subcultures which are good at the subversive element – calling people to repent and believe. Other evangelical subcultures concentrate on the fulfilment aspect – focusing on the felt needs that are met in the gospel or the God-shaped hole in every heart. We need to do both: to expose people's idolatry and point to the true fulfilment of hopes and desires.

Evangelizing the heart[2]

We have already seen that the culture of the urban poor commonly has the following characteristics:

- non-abstract, concrete thinking
- non-literate, oral learning
- non-diary, relational lifestyles

Many of the 'tried-and-tested' models of evangelism have been honed on university campuses. Among students and graduates, they have proved effective. But transport these same methods to working-class and deprived areas, and you may find yourself answering questions that no-one is asking. We need to learn how to speak the gospel in ways that connect with the ordinary lives of people from working-class and deprived areas. 'We need an apologetic,' says Dai Hankey, 'for ganja, for benefit fraud, for sex outside of marriage, for Facebook gossip, because these are the issues with which people are going to be struggling.'

According to the Bible, *the source of all human behaviour and emotions is the heart.* The 'heart' here is not simply the organ that pumps blood round the body. Nor is it the seat of emotions, in contrast to our reason. In our culture, we think with our heads and feel with our hearts. But, in the Bible, the seat of the emotions is as often as not your bowels (in the sense that we might speak of 'our gut feeling' or 'stomach-churning fear'). Instead, the heart refers to the inner person or my essential self. It is shorthand for our thinking and desires. We both feel with our hearts *and* think with our hearts. Our hearts experience hope and fear and love and longing. All our actions flow from the heart.

> Above all else, guard your heart,
>   for it is the wellspring of life.
> (Proverbs 4:23)

The heart is the wellspring or fountain of our lives, our motivational core. Our lives, our words, our actions, our emotions are all the outflow of what is going on in our hearts. (See also Mark 7:20–23; Luke 6:43–45; Romans 1:21–25; Ephesians 4:17–24; James 4:1–10.) Circumstances, upbringing, hormones and our personal history all play a part in shaping our behaviour, but the root problem is the sinful desires of the heart (James 1:13–15).

Our hearts experience hope and fear and love and longing. All our actions flow from the heart.

Hebrews 4:12 speaks of 'the thoughts and attitudes of the heart'. There are two core activities in the heart, from which all else flows: what we think or believe, and what we desire or worship. Destructive behaviour and negative emotions arise because we choose to trust other interpretations instead of God's Word, and because we choose to worship other gods instead of God (what the New Testament calls 'the lusts of the flesh' or 'the sinful desires of the heart'). A sinful desire is not just a desire for a bad thing. It can also be a desire for a good thing, which has become bigger than God. To want a job, for example, is a good thing. But if my unemployment makes me depressed, then my desire for employment has grown too big – bigger than my desire for God – so that I cannot be content with God's sovereignty over my life. Our idols are usually a reflection of our fundamental idolatry of self. We worship ourselves instead of worshipping God. Even when we make an idol of other people, it is commonly because we crave their approval or fear their rejection. We want them to affirm (= worship) us. Sinful acts always have this characteristic: they have their origin in lies about God and lies about ourselves. Sinful acts are always the result of some form of unbelief.

This offers a point of connection with people, a hook, an opportunity to engage. People may not feel guilt, but they do feel trapped. Jesus says, 'Everyone who sins is a slave to sin' (John 8:34). Idolatry and unbelief lead to slavery: we become trapped in our sins. The thing that our hearts treasure or worship will be the thing that controls our lives (Matthew 6:21, 24). The gods we create will become our masters. People feel trapped in their negative behaviour or negative emotions. The gospel is good news of freedom from the enslavement to the addictive behaviour and negative emotions created by sinful desires.

But when Jesus said that everyone who sins is a slave to sin, he also said, 'The truth will set you free' (John 8:31–34). If I am enslaved by my worries, then freedom is found in trusting in the sovereign care of my heavenly Father. If I am enslaved by the need to prove myself, then freedom is found in trusting that I am fully justified in God's sight through the atoning work of Christ.

Consider the woman at the well in Samaria, in John 4. Jesus promises her living water that will truly satisfy. Then he appears to head off at a tangent by asking her to bring her husband. But this question leads straight to her heart. She says she has no husband to fetch. Like Israel drinking mud from broken cisterns in Jeremiah 2, this woman has been looking for meaning and satisfaction in marriage, sex and intimacy. But they are like water that leaves her thirsty again. She then tries to change the subject, with her question about worship, but Jesus uses it to go right to the heart of the issue. The issue is not *where* you worship, but *what* you worship. She was trying to find satisfaction from a man instead of from God and, in the process, had made an idol of sexual intimacy. Jesus, of course, has supernatural knowledge of her heart and her history.

We often have the advantage of spending time with people and discovering the desires that drive their behaviour. Shane Goodyear, from Roehampton in south London, emphasizes the importance of listening to people, 'even if they go on for hours'. We can see patterns in their lives. In the case of the woman at the well, the maths tells the story: five husbands plus another man. What are the patterns in people's lives? Are the words: 'If only . . . ' a refrain?

When talking to someone, we need to ask ourselves, first, what do they believe about God? In other words, what are the lies that enslave them at a functional level? Secondly, what do they want more than God? Or, what are the desires that enslave them at a functional level? We need to ask questions that expose enslaving desires. Then our proclamation of truth can be relevant and personal. So we need to explore what people are wanting or worshipping, and what they are thinking or believing, in those moments when they feel enslaved, angry, bitter, frustrated, unsatisfied, desperate and so on. We need to look for topics that generate energy, make them excited, agitated, enthusiastic. These will often be windows onto the things they care most deeply about. Ask people: 'What do you want?'; 'Why?'; 'Why does it matter so much?'

Behind every presenting issue are lies and desires that enslave, together with an opportunity to proclaim truth that liberates, and desires (or worship) that liberate.

- lies that enslave ⇨ truth that liberates
- desires that enslave ⇨ desires (worship) that liberate

It is the specific ways in which the truth of the gospel counters the underlying lies of sin of different individuals that offer us an opportunity to present the gospel to the urban poor. Pete Jackson from Kendray in Barnsley says, 'Many issues can't be hidden. And when things are out in the open, there's an opportunity to explain how much of what makes up our messy lives – and I include myself – are just symptoms of a bigger problem, namely our turning away from and ignoring God. Address that first, and the others issues will, in time, be taken care of.'

One of the dangers for middle-class outreach in deprived areas is that the workers become advice-givers. But advice does not save anyone. Of course, sometimes giving advice is an appropriate act of love. But it can all too easily become patronizing. Worse still, it can communicate a message of morality about how you clean up your life. We are in the business of proclaiming the good news of a Liberator.

One of the potential weaknesses of some evangelistic methods is that they can leave a person's idolatrous desires untouched. People assent to certain truths, but they do not engage with the heart change required. Gospel presentations and apologetic answers can sometimes merely convert people to facts (assent). A heart-centred approach converts people to Christ (living faith).

But a heart-centred approach is particularly appropriate for the poor for two reasons.

First, the poor often lack the veneer of respectability, and the resources to cover up their idolatries. As a result, they live messy lives. There is less hiding and less pretending. This is what makes work among the poor exciting. People are more real. Their lives are open – open in the sense that their sins are on the table, as it were, and open in the sense that their crises bring an openness to change. They are like the people Paul describes in 1 Corinthians 1:26–31 who shame the wise, powerful and rich. We are all captivated or captured by our sinful desires. Crisis moments bring these desires to the surface and expose our slavery.

Secondly, this approach engages with specifics, and people are more likely to engage with the particular issues that affect their lives. (You are controlled by your desire for a sexual partner; Jesus can set you free. Or you self-harm because of the guilt you feel; Jesus offers you lasting forgiveness.) People come with presenting issues: anger, bitterness, parenting, shopping, addiction, economic need, depression, violence and so on. We can do more than deal with these *as a context* for speaking the gospel, which treats them as separate issues: I help sort out someone's housing benefit, in the hope that I might then have an opportunity to give them a gospel presentation or invite them to church. Instead, I can treat these presenting issues directly so they become ways into heart issues. We need to connect the gospel with the specifics of people's lives, rather than, or as well as, starting with big metaphysical questions.

We need to contextualize the gospel for the urban poor. But, in effect, we need to contextualize the gospel on a person-by-person basis – to working-class and middle-class people alike. We can identify the particular sinful desires that control a person's life and the particular truth that will set them free.

To help apply this heart-centred approach, here are two frameworks.

1. Four points of intersection
We are all interpreters, and we are all looking for interpretations of life. American pastor and author Paul Tripp says,

When we say that God designed human beings to be
interpreters we are getting to the heart of why human beings
do what they do. Our thinking conditions our emotions, our
sense of identity, our view of others, our agenda for the
solution of our problems, and our willingness to receive
counsel from others. That is why we need a framework for
generating valid interpretations that help us respond to life
appropriately. Only the word of the Creator can give us that
framework.[3]

Human beings are crying out for some sort of interpretation.
We often bemoan our lack of opportunities to witness to
unbelievers, but, if witness involves the interpretation of life,
then all of life becomes a witnessing opportunity. If you think
about how conversations develop, they often involve looking
for interpretations, or offering interpretations, or looking for
interpretations to be confirmed. Isn't that right? 'Innit' (*sic*) is
a request to have an interpretation of the world confirmed.
Our conversations are littered with opportunities to engage
with interpretations of life.

We were made to understand the world around us through
God's Word. But our rebellion against God began when,
encouraged by the serpent in the Garden of Eden, we questioned that interpretation. We questioned whether God's reign
was really good. We wondered whether we would be better off
without him. Life unravels when we believe other interpretations instead of God's Word.

The primary way in which people interpret life is through
stories. Everyone has a gospel story, their version of salvation.
We can use the framework of creation, fall, redemption
and consummation as four points of intersection – four
points at which people's stories intersect with the gospel
story.

Creation	my identity
Fall	my problem
Redemption	my solution
Consummation	my hope

Here are a couple of examples of 'gospel stories' that people might use to interpret their lives:

Creation	I need to be loved.
Fall	My problem is, I don't get the love I need.
Redemption	My solution is to offer my body to people, so that they love me.
Consummation	My hope is that having sex will make me feel loved and complete.

Creation	I need respect.
Fall	My problem is, I am vulnerable to verbal and physical attack.
Redemption	My solution is to carry a knife.
Consummation	My hope is that violence will make me respected.

Identifying these attitudes in terms of creation, fall, redemption and consummation highlights the points of intersection with the true gospel of Jesus. Here are the opportunities to speak of the Bible story to the people we meet.

Often those opportunities will arise when people's interpretations of life break down. Obviously, it is rare for someone to say, 'My interpretation of life no longer adds up', or 'I think my interpretation of life may be enslaving.' But unbelievers are saying it all the time in different ways, if we only have ears to hear it. In the case of the first example, a woman may be offering herself in sex to men, but realize she is not actually finding love or happiness. Our job is to listen out for failing interpretations or idolatrous desires, and rephrase them as beliefs about God. Then we can tell the true gospel story.

The gospel is richly textured, so the true gospel story can be told in a variety of ways that intersect with the specifics of people's lives. The following version of the true gospel story is designed to speak to the woman who feels the need to be loved.

Creation	I need to be loved ⇨
	I am made to love God.
Fall	My problem is, I don't get the love I need ⇨
	My problem is, I love myself more than God and look elsewhere for love.
Redemption	My solution is to offer my body to people, so that they love me ⇨
	My solution is to stop loving myself and love the one who gave his body for me on the cross.
Consummation	My hope is that having sex will make me feel loved and complete ⇨
	My hope is an everlasting relationship with God, in which I love and am loved.

Most of the time, we will not get the opportunity to tell all four stages of the true gospel story in one go. But we can reiterate one. We may often need to trust in the sovereignty of God in salvation, and patiently wait for God to give us further opportunities to fill out the story.

In a recent conversation with a homeless man, my friend said, 'What you're really saying is that drink is your saviour.' This is a redemption statement (or rather a statement of *failed* redemption). The homeless man was doing circular thinking, so he kept coming back and repeating this: 'My problem is, I think drink is my saviour.' It's not difficult to take this on: 'Drink's a pretty rubbish saviour, isn't it? It's such a temporary solution. It actually makes things worse. Jesus is a much better Saviour. He doesn't wreck your life; he wrecks his life in your place, to set you free.'

Common alternative stories[4]

The victim
Identity   I'm a victim.
Problem   Other people have given me a hard time.
Solution   I fight back or moan.
Fruit   I'm worn out or paranoid.

Typical evangelistic conversation:
Sometimes I feel like I'm a victim, and that life's so hard. And I try to fight back. But it wears me out. But I've found another way to deal with it. I go to God now instead, and I give him my complaint. I trust that he will take care of it. So I chill, because Jesus gives me rest.

The boss
Identity   I'm in charge.
Problem   Other people don't do what I want.
Solution   I need to make other people change, so I can be happy.
Fruit   I'm never satisfied, and I lose friendships.

Typical evangelistic conversation:
Sometimes I find myself wishing everyone around me would change, and then I'd be happy. But when I try to make other people change, I fall out with them. But the Bible says I'm the

---

person who needs to change. The way I treat God needs to change, and the way I treat other people needs to change. Life really is better with God in charge. And I've found that God will forgive me, even though I need to change, and he'll help me change.

The party person

Identity   I'm a party animal.

Problem   I don't get enough pleasure.

Solution   I need to get pleasure at every possible opportunity, so I can be happy.

Fruit   I'm never satisfied and I do things I know I shouldn't really do, things that hurt me and other people.

Typical evangelistic conversation:

I used to think that I'd be happy if I drank enough and went raving more. But many Sundays after partying, I felt sad. I never felt truly satisfied that way. Now I get satisfaction from God – and it's way better. Now I have real peace.

2. Four liberating truths

Underlying people's behaviour and emotions are lies about God. 'God gave them over in the sinful desires of their hearts to sexual impurity for the degrading of their bodies with one another,' says Paul. Why? 'They exchanged the truth of God for a lie, and worshipped and served created things rather than the Creator – who is for ever praised. Amen' (Romans 1:24–25). Because untruths about God underlie people's behaviour, their behaviour gives us opportunities to speak the truth about him. And because lies about God lead to enslaving behaviour, we have an opportunity to speak *liberating* truth that people will hear as good news. So it is helpful to keep in mind the following four liberating truths:[5]

1. God is great – so we don't have to be in control
2. God is glorious – so we don't have to fear others
3. God is good – so we don't have to look elsewhere
4. God is gracious – so we don't have to prove ourselves

These truths offer a diagnostic kit to help identify which lies about God are behind presenting issues. They also allow us to identify how the gospel offers good news in those situations. A failure to believe one of these four broad truths will account for most of the negative behaviour and emotions that we encounter. If we can show people how their idolatrous desires control their lives, then we can present the truth of the gospel as good news and articulate a reason why they should welcome the message of Jesus.

When people complain about the local council, for example, Shane Goodyear speaks of God's sovereignty over the council: 'The failings of officials will be judged by God, but then so will yours, apart from grace in Christ.'

If I meet someone who is manipulative or worried about life, then I can say, 'Here is good news – you don't have to be in control, because God is in control.'

If I meet someone who is enslaved by other people's opinions, who fears rejection or craves respect, then I can say, 'Here is good news – you don't have to fear others, because God is glorious, and he smiles upon you.'

If I meet someone who is enslaved by the pursuit of wealth or pleasure or sex, I can say, 'Here is good news – you don't have to look elsewhere, because God is good, and to know him is true joy.'

If I meet someone who is desperate to prove herself or make it in life or look down on others, I can say, 'Here is good news – you don't have to prove yourself, because God is gracious, and Christ has done it all.'

Tracy often asked for parenting advice. She was a single mother, struggling to cope with four children. At first, we directed her to SureStart parenting courses. But Tracy never completed the programmes – her life was too chaotic to attend regular weekly sessions. But we also realized that we were missing a gospel opportunity. So instead, when she talked about parenting, we gave her tips on discipline, but we also started to talk about heart issues, the rebellious attitude of her children and the need for everyone to learn to live under authority. We talked about the way our selfish desires as parents (for control, for respect, for comfort) skews our discipline, making it self-centred rather than an act of love for our children. This then led to conversations about living under God's authority, about finding identity in Christ rather than in parental success, and about our need for Jesus to set us free from our selfishness.

After the birth of her fourth child, Tracy started experiencing panic attacks. It was not the first time in her life that she had experienced them. Her mother had spent significant periods in psychiatric hospital, so Tracy had a strong fear that she might go the same way. Her mother's mental ill health meant that Tracy had spent much of her teenage years in (or running away from) care homes. As a result, Tracy also had a strong fear of social services taking her children away from her. With the birth of her fourth child, she began to harbour dark thoughts about harming the baby. She wondered whether these were from the devil, and whether the devil might make her hurt her children.

For several weeks, she phoned me almost every day, seeking reassurance. We developed a number of 'slogans' that we would repeat to each other. 'Not "what if" but "what is" – and "what is" is that God is in control'; 'God is greater than your thoughts and God is greater than Satan'; 'Yesterday was a victory; today is a new battle.' This growing realization of God's sovereignty not only kept Tracy going and gradually brought relief from her fears, but it also led to a new realization of the centrality of God and his glory. It brought her into a new and more direct relationship with God. In the past, Tracy had related to the church, but not really to God himself. Now she is talking about the need to change her self-centredness and live for God.

Conclusion

Evangelizing the heart through the four points of intersection and the four liberating truths enables us to offer specific relief for specific issues. But we are actually doing much more. We are using presenting issues as a window on the heart. The gospel impacts the day-to-day realities of people's lives. Because of this, the day-to-day realities of life create opportunities to speak of the big gospel story. We are not simply meeting felt needs. Instead, we are using felt needs to reveal underlying slaveries and idolatries. We are inviting people to believe the good news.

5 DISCIPLESHIP IN WORKING-CLASS AND DEPRIVED AREAS

Discipling people from working-class and deprived areas requires real commitment. Many leaders struggle to keep those who make professions of faith. Years of hurt and deprivation retain a strong influence, even after conversion. A church full of broken people can absorb many of the church's resources, leaving little time for evangelism. Unlike middle-class contexts, the local neighbourhood may not produce many natural leaders or organizers who can quickly exercise leadership when they are converted. Forming a group of broken individuals into a grounded, missional, loving, attractive community can at times feel like an impossible task. It certainly cannot be done from the safety of a study.

One such church has seen only one man baptized in the last ten years. They do everything they can to make church appeal to men, emphasizing strong male figures, organizing male-oriented activities, talking of Jesus as the man we want to be, and so on. But it is the women who come, perhaps because they are willing to admit their need. One man first sat on the steps outside the church, then on a chair by the back door, and only after that at the back among the congregation. This creates a problem for leaders. They desperately want to grow other leaders from within. But, in their context, men do not seem to mature until their mid-thirties. Before that, they may be working and have children, but their only real interests are football and computer games. Only later do they start to get bored with a life that consists merely of Xbox, beer and football.

Scrambled-egg churches

Particular difficulties in discipleship arise from:

- the legacies of abuse, addiction or mental illness
- conflict in family and relationships
- a victim mentality or a passive sense of entitlement
- negative responses to people who are different
- the 'need' for respect
- life strategies that include escapism and a tendency to live for the moment
- unreliability
- problems in grasping the character of God, especially his loving authority

A number of Welsh pastors have started to refer to their churches as 'scrambled-egg' churches:

> Some churches are poached-egg churches – clean, tidy and predictable. The white stays white, the yellow stays yellow, and it all fits snugly on the neat square of toast. If ketchup is involved, it is

placed to the side of the toast for dipping. However, in scrambled-egg churches, the white, yellow and the ketchup are all mashed up together. These are the kinds of churches in which all sorts of people, with all sorts of problems, can come and meet Jesus in the midst of a community of believers who embrace the sanctified chaos of the gospel in the real world.

In these churches, struggles tend to be in the open. Crises will be common. Meetings do not feel polished. People do not commit to regular activities. Andy Mason has done one-to-one Bible studies with many people on the World's End estate where he works, but few will actually come to church. If you are pastoring a scrambled-egg church, it can feel as if you are constantly fire-fighting. Julian Rebera from Moulsecoomb in Brighton says,

> The potential for growth is limited. People who have come into the church are so messed up that they don't model the kind of community we want to attract people into. They struggle with acceptance. They want to resolve problems with a punch-up. There are few good, strong believers who are modelling godly Christian manhood or community. It has taken fourteen years of graft, and we have maybe twenty-five people who can model community.

But there are also many blessings associated with this kind of church. Conflict may be associated with aggression, but it is, as we've seen, often on the surface, where it can be swiftly addressed. Grace can be enacted week by week, in ways that powerfully model the gospel. Broken people can feel welcome, without having to achieve a level of respectability.

So what principles will help us as we disciple people in working-class and deprived areas? The foundational principle is that we pastor people with the gospel.

Disciple with the gospel

The gospel is not simply the A-B-C of the Christian life, but the A-to-Z of the Christian life, as Tim Keller has reminded us.[1] In other words, we are not simply converted by the gospel and then expected to continue through other means. We become Christians, continue as Christians and grow as Christians through the gospel. This truth is of special help when pastoring in deprived areas, for a number of reasons.

1. One gospel for believers and unbelievers

When people are converted from backgrounds in which the effects and brokenness of sin are deeply embedded, change will take time. This means that it can often be unclear whether someone is a Christian or not. But our message is the same, whether they are a believer or an unbeliever: the gospel. We evangelize with the gospel and we disciple with the gospel. This is liberating and something that makes pastoral work clearer. Obviously, nothing is more important for the person concerned than whether he or she is a Christian or not. But as the pastor, we do not need to resolve this before we can speak into their lives. If someone is an unbeliever, we will speak the gospel, and if they are a believer, we will speak the gospel. So, however complicated it may be to discern their status before God, our role is clear. We cannot go wrong if we address people's presenting issues with the gospel.

We become Christians, continue as Christians and grow as Christians through the gospel.

The four points of intersection and the four liberating truths outlined in the last chapter can be used just as well as we disciple one another with the gospel. In this way, we can begin to disciple people, even before they have confessed faith in Christ.

2. Following Jesus before respectability

We are trying to create followers of Jesus, not middle-class individuals. We are not trying to produce respectability as defined by middle-class culture, any more than we are trying to produce people worthy of respect as defined by the culture of deprived areas. Remember, Jesus was not regarded as respectable by the mainstream culture of his day.

One example of where we can easily impose middle-class norms is in the areas of regularity and punctuality. We've already noted the lack of a diary lifestyle. And those who have never held down a regular job can find punctuality and regularity an alien concept. The problem is that church activities are often structured around programmes and diaries, and regular church attendance may not be seen as an obvious obligation. Also, being part of a home group will not come naturally in a culture in which people do not belong to clubs. One church planter finds that his congregation are willing to meet for a Bible study, but less willing to commit to being routinely with the same people in a home group. Here are people who might often visit their extended family, but would not dream of arranging to meet with them each Tuesday at 7.30. It's hardly surprising that they are likely to feel the same way about the church family.

Another example is attitudes towards anger. Anger can be righteous. God himself expresses anger. Human beings, however, are more often angry for unrighteous reasons or in unrighteous ways. But there are also class differences in the way we express and interpret anger. One church planter says, only partly tongue-in-cheek, that if you want to appear godly in middle-class church circles, you just need to talk quietly. Volatility is suspect. In contrast, among working-class individuals, open displays of anger are more acceptable. Even a pint after a punch-up is not uncommon. So it is important to ensure that our understanding of anger is formed by the Bible rather than by our social background. You may find open displays of anger or conflict difficult to handle, but it is important to seek to address the real issue, rather than merely contain external displays. Some outbursts may seem out of proportion to the offence caused. But remember that a person may be carrying years of suppressed resentment or guilt. The latest offence is merely the trigger for pent-up pain. If you just respond to the immediate cause, you may miss the opportunity to address a long-standing heart issue.

In what ways might new converts in your church be tempted to change as a result of social pressure rather than in response to the gospel? In what ways do you feel tempted to cultivate respectability more than heart change in your congregation?

This is how Shane Goodyear describes what it should look like to be a Christian in a contextually appropriate way on his estate:

> Laying down your life for your brothers and sisters. Being there for people. Ready to lend to people if they need it. Putting yourself out for people. Ringing one another up. Praying for one another. (The other day, a believer struggling with assurance rang up after midnight.) Holiness is love. A different attitude to time and money. You should provide for your pastor – even if it's just £1.

3. Heart change before behaviour change

We want people's behaviour to change. Conversion should lead to a radical change in behaviour and priorities. We are called to be holy just as God is holy (1 Peter 1:16). We need to be bold and clear, as we call people to turn from sin. Indeed, we can often be more confrontational in working-class and deprived areas, where middle-class norms of polite circumlocution do not apply. People expect you to say what you mean and mean what you say.

One pastor delivers what he calls a 'hand grenade' in his Sunday sermon, and then spends the rest of the week encouraging, teaching and counselling, where this is needed. In his sermons, he does not hold back from the challenge of God's Word, even when he knows that this will directly confront sin. He finds that, if he then allows his congregation some time and space, they will work out the implications for themselves. This does not mean people taking notes that they later pray through over a coffee. The key time for working out application for many is while standing smoking outside, after the Sunday service.

But our calls for behaviour change must flow from heart change. Behaviour change on its own is merely legalism. We cannot chivvy people into holiness. We need to apply the gospel to their hearts. Our goal is a love for God and his people, an assurance of God's fatherly love, a joy in Christ, an attitude of continual repentance, and restored relationships. Only this kind of heart change will produce real and lasting behavioural change.

Addressing specific behaviours creates opportunities to go after heart issues. Someone who loses his temper will have done so because deep-seated desires have been threatened or thwarted. What we need is not a neat pastoral programme, but 'freestyle pastoring', in which we respond to events as they arise.

Andy Mason in World's End, London, finds it helpful to take a step back from particular behavioural issues. He counsels believers, 'I'm not talking to you about this *behaviour*, but *the lordship of Christ*.' He reminds them that being a Christian is about a total change in allegiance to Christ. This does not diminish the gravity of the sin. Rather, by bringing it into a relational focus, it highlights how personal and offensive to God a person's sin is. So addressing the particular behaviour leads directly into a discussion about the heart attitude towards God.

4. God's Word of gospel before my word of advice

It is all too easy, when working with people whose lives are dysfunctional, to get drawn into giving advice. To some extent, of course, this is a natural and loving thing to do.

One danger, however, is that we start to adopt a parental tone.

Childlike tone[2]	Parental tone	Adult tone
defensive, whining, victimized, playful, curious	*authoritative, judgmental, demanding, supportive, loving*	*non-judgmental, factual, questioning*
'Stop getting at me.' 'Nobody likes me.' 'I hate you.' 'It's all your fault.' 'Don't blame me.'	'You should do this.' 'Just get on with it.' 'That's so immature.' 'Why can't you be like her?'	'What can we do about this?' 'Can I recommend something?' 'What are your choices?' 'What's going to happen if you do that?' 'That's not how I see it.'

Adopting a parental tone clearly creates problems. It can sound – rightly or wrongly – as if we are judging those we are address-ing to be incompetent. It encourages the hearer in return to adopt a parental tone, which may then sound sarcastic or create conflict, or to adopt a childlike role, which means that they respond with childish behaviour or subservience, something that only reinforces their powerlessness. So it is important to speak to people as equals, as fellow adults.

The more fundamental problem with the focus on advice-giving is that it can replace or confuse gospel proclamation. What this person needs is not just improved life strategies, but a Redeemer. Indeed, what will bring lasting change is the change of heart produced by the gospel. If we are not careful, our advice-giving can be interpreted as a call to good works or respectability.

We can instead:

- Look for opportunities to ask for advice. Everyone will have knowledge which they can impart to us, from how to mend a car to which areas to avoid at night.
- Look for opportunities to move from advice to proclamation. We can do this by identifying the heart issues that underlie the need for advice.
- Carefully distinguish between our limited word of advice and God's authoritative Word of gospel.

5. Grace, grace, grace

We need constantly to emphasize grace. Even as we call people to godliness, we need to remind them that God will forgive his children if they fall. It is all too common for people to refrain from a particular sin for a while, before falling once more. They may then try to hide the fact that they have sinned, or be too ashamed to continue attending church. What drags them back into their old way of life is not falling into sin per se, but the failure to believe in grace after their fall.

Grace, of course, does not minimize sin – quite the opposite. We only grasp the full extent of God's amazing grace as we grasp the full horror of our sin. So, in a grace-centred church, there will be challenge and rebuke. Sin will not be excused or minimized. We need to create church cultures in which grace means being open about struggles, and confessing sin. Then, as sin is challenged and confessed, the forgiveness and acceptance of God can be proclaimed, and find expression in the forgiveness and acceptance of his people.

6. Pray, pray, pray
We cannot change anyone. People will not be liberated from their slaveries and idolatries through our counselling methodologies or apologetic arguments or orthodox doctrine. It is God who changes people, through the work of his Son and the power of his Spirit. We cannot correlate inputs and outputs in a mechanistic way. We need to emphasize the role of the Spirit, expect divine intervention in hearts and lives, and pray for miraculous provision and change.

What level of change should we expect?
A common question for Christians working in deprived areas is what level of change they should expect and over what period of time. As we've seen, because we speak the gospel both to believers and unbelievers, we do not need to discern a person's status before we speak to them. But discerning whether someone is a Christian is still important when it comes to offering assurance or deciding whether to baptize him or her. Do you baptize someone if she has stopped swearing, but is still using drugs? Or if he has stopped sleeping around, but is still cheating on his benefits? What about someone who professes Christ, but is still getting drunk? When do you exercise church discipline? There are no straightforward answers. But here are some considerations.

1. Jesus said that, before a person builds a tower or a king goes to war, they must count the cost (Luke 14:25–33).

In the same way, before someone becomes a Christian, they must count the cost. So our evangelism must include a call to repentance, to a change of allegiance and to submission to Christ. And we need to spell out what this will mean for people in the specifics of their lives. One church leader says,

> People don't have a problem with 'Jesus is Lord'. But this doesn't always follow through to their lives. People learn about the lordship of Christ in very specific areas. Sex, suffering, alcohol – their theology and conversion is in the specific issues, not in the abstract.

Jesus tells the rich young ruler, 'Sell everything you have and give to the poor' (Luke 18:22). This is not how most of us are taught to answer the question: 'What must I do to inherit eternal life?' (Luke 18:18)! But Jesus makes repentance specific, forcing the young man to choose between God and money. We cannot pull out the small print once someone has become a Christian, emphasizing the free grace of God before conversion and only talking about moral changes once they are 'in'. The evangelistic pitch of Jesus was: 'Any of you who does not give up everything he has cannot be my disciple' (Luke 14:33). The person who responds to this call may continue to fall into sin many times, but the fundamental orientation of their lives will have changed. Andy Mason says, 'I identify something in someone's life and say, "If you become a Christian that's got to change." By picking on one thing, I'm going after their heart. "If it comes down to your will versus Jesus' will, who will win?"' Dai Hankey says, 'You need to show people that they cannot say, "I'll give Jesus my heart, but I want to carry on doing this." That's not giving your heart to Jesus. Jesus died for your sin. To want to carry on in sin is to continue doing that for which Christ died.'

2. The important thing is an attitude of repentance and the direction of travel.

A key distinguishing mark of Christians is not whether we sin or not, but how we respond to correction. So we should give more weight to a person's response when they sin than to their behaviour, as their response will be more symptomatic of their heart attitude.

3. Change takes a lifetime for every believer.

But for people in working-class and deprived areas, progress can often seem slower. It may feel like they are taking more steps backwards than forwards. Dysfunctional families, a poor experience of the educational system, mental illness, the passivity of a social-welfare culture, lack of opportunity, addictions – all, as we've seen, can produce deep-seated issues. Middle-class individuals come to Christ with an expectation that change is possible, because they are part of a culture of success. People in deprived areas have learned not to have pretensions, nor to expect change. So we need to remember that sanctification is progressive, and celebrate the change that is actually taking place.

A newly converted couple suddenly went off the radar of a church plant. The church leader did not see them for a while, but was well aware of their chaotic lifestyle and the couple's violent rows. A few months later, they came back to church, bringing the woman's sister. What had struck the church leader as wholly inappropriate behaviour had struck her as remarkable. She could not believe that her sister had not walked out on her husband and gone to stay with her mother or friends. She knew this was what would have happened in the past, so she recognized that something had radically changed in her sister's life. She wanted to know more.

4. You don't need to address every issue at once.

Dai Hankey says,

Often there's a list of issues, and you can't address them all at the same time. God doesn't deal with every issue in my life all at the same time. So think prayerfully about where to start. We often tell people, 'Getting saved is like giving Jesus the keys to your house. Every room is filthy. Sanctification is going to involve Jesus cleaning up, room by room.' Often in this situation they respond, 'You mean things like . . . ' This is the Holy Spirit bringing conviction. So this gives us an agenda for change.

5. We are not only sinners; we also live surrounded by other sinners.

We are sinners, and we are sinned against. Some people emphasize that the poor are sinned against. This has the appearance of compassion, but in fact it offers no hope, because they remain passive victims of others' actions. Some emphasize only that people are sinners. But this, too, lacks compassion, failing to recognize the pain that people experience and the way this shapes their behaviour. It fails to recognize the impact of dysfunctional families and their surrounding culture (what the Bible calls 'the world').

One church planter struggled to feel compassion for a seven-year-old boy on his estate who was out of control. The boy would smash things up, got expelled from local schools and even exposed himself at Sunday school. While out walking his dog late one night, the church planter came across the boy in the middle of a dark street. His father could be seen in the distance, swearing at the boy's grandmother: 'I don't want him to come near me!' Although the boy's behaviour has not changed, this window onto the boy's life has allowed this church planter to feel compassion. The boy is indeed a sinner, but he is also sinned against.

6. The sins of those from deprived areas are often readily apparent (addiction, rage, theft, extramarital sex, drunkenness). We've already seen that the sins of the middle classes, in contrast, are typically less immediately apparent (greed, pride,

self-reliance, individualism, lack of generosity, self-justification).
Indeed, many 'middle-class sins' produce behaviours that, in
and of themselves, are commendable (hard work, honesty, self-
control), but which may reflect attitudes of self-righteousness,
self-reliance or self-fulfilment. Again, we need to celebrate the
change that is taking place, without measuring people against
some false standard of middle-class respectability.

7. The questions: 'Do you believe?' and 'Have you repented?'
can too easily get mired in issues of intellectual understanding
and the extent of change. Often more helpful questions
are: 'Do you love Jesus?' or 'Do you need Jesus?' or 'Do
you want to obey Jesus?' These questions go straight to the
heart.

A new community

The first two days after conversion are crucial in any new
Christian's life. This is the common experience of church
leaders working in deprived areas. You cannot wait until the
next time the church meets together. 'You can lose them in
those two days,' says Simon Smallwood from Dagenham.
People return to friends, families, gangs whose influence is
persuasive. However dysfunctional such groups may be, they
offer a sense of community and belonging. So, in the early
days of a new believer's new life, it is important to look for
any opportunity to spend time with him or her. And it may
also be important for them to avoid old influences at this
early stage.

One convert from a high-rise estate avoids his previous
sexual partners and will not be alone with a woman. Coming
from a culture that does not know social drinking, he has also
stopped attending pubs. To replace these old communities, the
church needs to offer new places of belonging and new spheres
of influence. The Sunday morning service and Wednesday

evening home group may not be enough. Duncan Forbes describes his own experiences:

> I saw friends and family as very important. My family hung out in the living room. My mates hung out in the pub or the street. When I was a young man, the church didn't seem to offer a decent alternative to this. They only met up on Sundays and Wednesday night. We now have our Bible study on Friday nights as an alternative to going out. There was a time when we had something available almost every night of the week. Sometimes I hang out with members of the church on the street, so that we are visible as a crew, rather than hidden away in the house. We encourage the church to be meeting up with one another regularly.

A convert from a deprived estate in London, a former drug user but now at university, is surprised by the lack of accountability in his new middle-class evangelical church. Regular confession of sin in a context of grace had been crucial for his growth as a believer. And in his home church on the estate, the members are often on the phone to one another, providing support and accountability.

How can you help someone from a deprived area to feel at home when they attend your meetings, if your church is predominantly middle class?

- give them a mug of tea
- sit with them
- explain everything
- introduce them to new people
- explain the culture clash if people appear snobby

If you can influence the meetings themselves, then try to make them less formal and scheduled, and try to ensure that they offer a tangible sense of God's presence, address real-life issues in the sermon and speak with passion to the heart. You may also need to think about mediating opportunities, contexts where someone can be involved in the network of church–community relationships before they attend a meeting.

Growing leaders

We lack leaders in working-class and deprived areas: many churches lack good leaders, and many areas lack churches. We need a new generation of church leaders and church planters. Many existing leaders have sacrificially come to serve from outside. Their role is important, and it would be great to see more like them. The experience of humble outsiders coming in to work alongside locals – not necessarily in salaried posts, but as active church members – has been very positive, for example, in St Andrew's Kendray in Barnsley. At the same time, we need to raise up leaders from deprived areas, those who know the culture and can model Christian maturity.

It is also possible to expect too little of people from deprived areas. Saul and Pilar Cruz, working in the slums of Mexico, found that workers from outside the slums were ineffectual, because they did not believe that people of the slums could change. Their solution was to grow their own leaders from among their converts, investing heavily in their lives. Now local Christians run the church and the transformation centre that they have established.

Raising up leaders from deprived areas may require us to rethink our image of a leader. As we've seen, most church leaders today are middle-class graduates with Bible college training. The apostles would not have met many of the criteria that some churches look for. Some, like Matthew, were literate, but most were uneducated. Only Paul could claim to have had formal theological training. Most were from humble backgrounds.

Clearly, class distinctions were very different in first-century Palestine from those of twenty-first-century Britain, but it is also clear that the disciples were viewed by their contemporaries as uneducated. Acts 4:13 says, 'When they saw the courage of Peter and John and realised that they were unschooled, ordinary men, they were astonished and they took note that these men had been with Jesus.' (More on this verse below.)

Paul had received the highest education possible. Of course, it is not a bad thing to be highly educated. But the criteria Paul uses for identifying Christian leaders are not skills-based, but character-based. The only skill needed is the ability to teach. For some, this will involve preaching, but this is not the only way the Bible is taught, and so it is not a necessary requirement for all leaders. The important thing is that leaders can apply God's Word to the life of the church and the lives of its members. The focus in 1 Timothy 3 and Titus 1 is on the character of the leader: their godliness, maturity and example.

Formal education commonly trains people to learn by creating logical frameworks or identifying abstract principles. Not only do people learn to learn in this way, but they also learn to *evaluate* learning in this way. In other words, they evaluate someone's understanding of the Bible in terms of their ability to create or reproduce abstract principles. The result is that many people are discounted and disenfranchised. The scary thought is that this might even include Jesus, were he on earth and teaching today!

Often the assumption is that leaders need theological training in a residential setting. For some, this may be appropriate. But it suits only a certain kind of person. It also tends to *create* a certain kind of person: academics who learn in highly literate ways and teach in literate ways. This model can shape our view of what it means to be a church leader and what we look for in potential church leaders.

A manual worker who hears the call to professional ministry is compelled to become an academic. He may have been leading people into Christian faith for decades . . . Churches of all denominations end up turning local leaders into 'puppets' who will conserve the old ways rather than 'prophets' who might lead God's people to new expressions of faith and witness.[3]

This is not how Jesus trained people, nor is it how Paul trained people. They trained people through apprenticeships, in the context of ministry. Roy Joslin concludes,

The best people to reach working-class folk with the gospel are working-class folk [themselves] . . . The indigenous church principle is particularly important in working-class communities. Parent churches or denominational bodies who neglect or choose to ignore this principle are likely to produce immature and over-dependent companies of working-class believers. They also perpetuate the long-held grievance that churches usually fail to give working men positions of status and responsibility. 'Church', like so many other things in working-class life, is run by 'them' for 'us'.[4]

Dai Hankey outlines the following ten principles for 'raising leaders from raw material':[5]

1. *We need to be praying faith-filled prayers* that God can and will raise up leaders from our communities. If he could use Peter, John and Levi, he can use anybody! In your community, who's the most messed-up, most notorious, most unlikely guy to ever get saved, let alone become a church leader? Why not commit to praying for him until that miracle happens?

2. *We need to view our people through the lens of faith*, not the lens of human reason. Just because they might not make the

cut in the posh Anglican church down the road, who's to say that they're not God's people to lead in your context? Is there anyone in your congregation right now who is beyond being set apart and used by God as a leader? No! We need to adjust our prayer lives accordingly.

3. *We need to be in this for the long haul.* Jesus spent three intensive years training his disciples. If we're going to believe that leaders can be home-grown in these areas, we need to be willing to count the cost and go the distance with them.

4. *We need to do micro as well as macro.* Jesus drew massive crowds, yet was willing to spend the majority of time with just twelve disciples. Are we willing to do the same? Raising leaders takes more than inspiring words on a Sunday. It involves putting in the hard yards behind the scenes with small groups and individuals.

5. *We need to encourage our people towards leadership*, through intentional teaching and discipleship.

6. *We need to share life with our people*, teaching them leadership through the example of our lives as well as our ministry.

7. *We need to create leadership opportunities.* It's not all about a direct leap from membership to eldership. Are there areas of responsibility into which we can release people that will set them off in the right direction? For example, we can begin by putting people on the refreshments rota or ask them to host (not necessarily lead) a Bible study.

8. *We need to give people grace when they fail.* And they will fail! We need to ensure that our churches process and address failure like Jesus did, as opposed to how the streets do it or how religious hypocrites do it.

9. *We need to lead in the light and hope of the resurrection.* If Christ can be raised from the grave, surely leaders can be raised from our estates.

10. *We need to plead with God for the Holy Spirit* to empower and
envision both ourselves and our people. Cultivating
strong, God-honouring leaders from the raw material
with which we're working is the only way to see
authentic churches planted and established in the
communities that we're serving. We need to be humble
enough to acknowledge that we don't have what it takes,
and allow the Holy Spirit to invade our lives and
churches in order to accomplish what only he can do.

Acts 4:13 says, 'When they saw the boldness of Peter and John,
and perceived that they were uneducated, common men, they
were astonished. And they recognized that they had been with
Jesus' (ESV). A pair of uneducated fishermen astonished the
religious elite. How did this happen? asks Dai. He continues,

> *They had been with Jesus.* This is a massive statement! Both these guys
> had been hand-picked by Jesus and had been with him ever since,
> sharing life, love and laughter together. They had learned from his
> teaching, witnessed his miracles, been trusted with responsibility,
> failed him miserably, but received grace.
>
> *And they were filled with the Spirit.* Only a short while before, Peter
> and John were not so bold, and they were not so astonishing! On the
> contrary, along with the other disciples, they had failed Jesus and fled.
> So what had changed for them? First, they had seen Jesus keep his
> promise to endure the cross and beat death. Secondly, they had
> received the immense gift that he had promised them before
> returning to glory – the Holy Spirit.

After being filled with the life-giving, power-infusing Spirit of
God, these men had been transformed for ever. They were
now ready to lead.

6 TEACHING THE WORD IN A NON-BOOK CULTURE

The gospel is at the heart of all change, and the Bible is the Spirit-inspired record of the gospel. So our ministries must be Word-centred. But how do we teach 'the Book' in a non-book culture? How do we proclaim the Word in a visual culture?

In a Church of England survey, new Christians made comments like: 'I am afraid to join a housegroup since I am a poor reader – silly reason, but true' or 'I would like to become more involved, but I feel as though I am not well enough educated.'[1] A feeling of shame or inadequacy tends to accompany these feelings, so that such comments may be infrequently heard, although frequently felt.

There is often a wide gap between church leaders (generally bookish people) and church members (generally not bookish people). Bible teaching often reflects styles of learning that suit bookish people, whether that be listening to a lecture or analysing the text of Scripture. We give people lots of things to read in our meetings: notices, hymn books, Bibles and so on. Non-book people can feel excluded.

By 'non-book people', we mean those who choose not to read, even though (usually) they can. It does *not* necessarily mean those who are unable to read, uneducated or unintelligent. As Gavin Reid says,

> It is important to note that we must not equate the ideas of being non-literary and not being intelligent. The two have no relationship. The factory worker may well be extremely intelligent and shrewd. He may even be able to grasp fairly complex ideas quickly without having to go through a logical sequence in his mind. He may well 'just see' what you are getting at. To write him off as simple because he is non-bookish is only to show the ignorance and short-sightedness of the literary type of person.[2]

The 'book' and 'non-book' categories do not map neatly on to middle-class and working-class categories. Some middle-class individuals are non-book, and many prefer oral approaches of learning. And many working-class people love to read (my grandmother being one example). There is a long history of self-improvement through literacy among working-class people, which finds expression in workers' libraries and organizations like the Workers' Education Association. Mez McConnell, for example, says that, while people in his area do not think in a linear way, they are bright and many of them do read.

There is nothing wrong with being a book person. Books are great. The problem arises when book learning dominates the way we do church and the way we teach the Bible. Christianity has been called 'the religion of the book'. Often, wanting to know more about the Bible has given people the impetus

Book people	Non-book people
We have lots of books.	We have work rooms.
We learn alone.	We learn in groups.
We take learning seriously.	We like a laugh.
We think in words.	We think in pictures.
We learn for the sake of learning.	We learn in order to do.
Our learning is structured.	We learn by doing.
We like to learn from an expert.	We like to learn from one another.
We structure our time by watches and diaries.	We structure our time by people and circumstance.

to learn to read, or start reading books. But it is also worth remembering that:

- Jesus taught and trained people without using a book.
- Most people in the early church probably could not read, and fewer still had access to the Scriptures.
- Being Word-centred is not the same as being book-centred.

Scholars estimate that literacy in Israel and Greece in the New Testament era was 3–12%, most likely around 5% percent. By 1750, still only 10% of world population was literate. Today 50% of the United States population prefer a non-literate approach to learning and decision-making. Half of these are illiterate.[3] People are talking of a growing 'secondary oral culture' tied to electronic media – for those who have learned to read, but get most of the important information in their lives through stories, via radio, TV, cinema and the internet.

A survey conducted by the National Year of Reading campaign and HarperCollins found that most people in the UK not only see reading as irrelevant, but find the world of books intimidating and unwelcoming. Lower-income, non-professional families (the C2DE socio-economic group) thought that readers were 'losers', 'at best loners', people 'who don't know how to live – an alien and unexciting tribe they seldom meet'. Honor Wilson-Fletcher, the Director of Reading for Life which conducted the survey, commented, 'There was no stigma or sense of loss – reading was simply not there. Reading has become associated with a certain area of population in terms of class and aspirations.' 'These are not families with literacy difficulties: they just do not read,' the survey noted. Reading was seen as isolating, while communal activities such as watching DVDs or playing computer games were valued more. The research found that, if people did enter a bookshop or library (and we might add, church), they found it 'acutely anxiety-inducing' and 'overwhelming'.[4]

Try the following exercise to see whether someone is more of a 'bookish' or a 'non-book' person.[5]

Book or non-book?

Which of these statements best describes you?

1. a. I like headings on a handout or screen when I'm listening to a talk
   b. I like pictures on a handout or screen when I'm listening to a talk

2. a. I usually plan a day out carefully
   b. I decide what to do on a day out as I go along

3. a. I have more books than DVDs
   b. I have more DVDs than books

4. a. I like to combine learning in a group with personal study
   b. I don't like studying on my own

5. a. I carefully think through decisions
   b. I act instinctively

6.a. When I visit someone with lots of books, I look through their shelves

  b. When I visit someone with lots of books, I feel intimidated

7.a. I have a filing system at home

  b. I have piles of paper around the home or a drawer full of paper

8.a. I see learning as an end in itself

  b. I'm only interested in learning how to do things

9.a. I read more books than magazines

  b. I read more magazines than books

10.a. I feel at home in a library or a bookshop

  b. I don't go to libraries and bookshops

11.a. I regulate my life by the clock

  b. I usually turn up when I'm ready

12.a. I value calm and objective reasoning

  b. I get emotionally involved in discussions

13.a. I like to talk about ideas

  b. I like to tell stories

14.a. When I get a new machine, I read the manual before switching it on

  b. When I get a new machine, I just start pressing buttons

If you answered mostly 'a' to the questions, then you are a bookish person.

If you answered mostly 'b' to the questions, then you are a non-book person.

In some contexts, the problem is in fact illiteracy. On one estate where a church is being planted, the rate of adult illiteracy is 48% (though the church planter also comments that people are often bright). More often than not, people can read, but do not connect with book-based learning.

In the world of work and school, what is known as the 'formal register' is expected. This employs standard sentence syntax and specific word choice. Researchers have found that most students from poor or minority backgrounds do not have access to the formal register at home and often cannot use it. Instead, they use the 'casual register', the language of friends and family, characterized by a 400- to 800-word vocabulary, in which word choice is not specific, sentence syntax is often incomplete and conversations are usually dependent upon non-verbal assists. The problem is that examinations are in formal register, and most well-paid jobs assume an ability to use formal register. Use the casual register in a job interview and you are out of the running. The same is true for leadership and theological education. It is possible to equate an inability to function in the formal register with a lack of godliness!

A related issue is that, in the formal register, it is usual to come straight to the point in a discussion. But, in the casual register, the pattern is to go around and around and finally get to the point (not unlike perhaps the Johannine writings).[6] There are two consequences of this.

First, people used to operating in the casual register can appear uninformed to those comfortable with the formal register, because they don't come straight to the point. 'For students who have no access to formal register, educators become frustrated with the tendency of these students to meander almost endlessly through a topic. It is simply the manner in which information is organized in casual register.'[7]

Secondly, it can appear as if people operating in the casual register do not have an opinion. Asked what they think, they may not provide a direct answer. If this is not recognized, then they may quickly become disenfranchised from church life, or it may be assumed they do not have leadership ability. But we want to operate with a principle of 'imbalanced mutual adaptation'. The urban poor may need to adapt as they move into leadership. But other people also need to adapt, by recognizing their patterns of discourse.

The power of sermons

We must not lose our nerve! We must still be Word-centred, because God rules through his Word and changes lives through his Word. People from working-class and deprived areas can listen well and follow an argument.

It is sometimes assumed that non-literate people prefer discussion groups to sermons. But the experience of the Reaching the Unreached working group suggests that the opposite is the case. For non-literate people, an interactive Bible study can be intimidating. It feels too much like an English comprehension exercise. We are invited to examine a text and answer text-based questions. Directions that lead away from the text (perhaps towards concrete application) are frowned upon. Even where the process is no longer intimidating, perhaps through familiarity, it does not feel reproducible by non-literate people.

Time and again, however, we have found that working-class people enjoy listening to sermons. They can cope with complex ideas just as well as anyone else. What they do not like is pretentious, academic or alien language. 'Don't patronize,' says Andy Mason. 'The men I'm with are not academic, but they are intelligent. I talk about the Greek of the original text, but I'll use plain rather than academic language.'

Interactive Bible studies also assume an attitude of dispassionate analysis – a typically middle-class approach to learning. Working-class people often relate better to the passionate exhortation of a sermon. They want to experience something. They value the tangible presence of God. This means that sermons need to address real-life issues. But more than this, it means that the sermon itself needs to be moving. Martyn Lloyd-Jones used to speak of the sermon accomplishing something in the moment. It is not just that a sermon imparts information that will be useful at some later date, but it brings heart change in the moment, as the preacher presents Christ in all his glory, beauty and grace. Evangelicalism perhaps needs to recover more of its traditional affirmation of the affections and experiential religion.

Steve Casey was preaching through Hosea. A woman who had just started coming to church asked for a Bible, so that she could read it for herself. She doesn't have any academic qualifications and doesn't have a bookshelf in her home. Yet, the very next day, when Steve asked how she was getting on, he was astonished to find she had read it all. 'What's it about?' he asked. 'It's showing us that God is faithful, even when his people aren't. I know all about unfaithfulness and how God must feel.' 'God's written Word is powerful, and people aren't as stupid as you think,' concludes Steve, 'so don't shy away from getting it into people's hands.'

One church in Mexico City found that people were intimidated when invited to 'read the Word of God'. They were not used to discussing texts. So the church now invites people to 'hear the voice of God'. The practice is the same – they read from the Bible and discuss its implications for their lives. But the language signals something more dynamic and inclusive than mere textual analysis.

We have found that using movie presentations and resources has worked well. Talking about a text is not something that is done in the wider culture, especially not in a home. But watching the television and discussing what you see is a normal part of day-to-day life, and feels much more natural. In other contexts, however, these resources have been less effective when they have been perceived to be middle class.

Non-book (and many bookish) people learn best when:

- Their own experience and knowledge are valued.
- They are able to learn through doing ('not reading the manual').
- Learning takes place through events, activities and unplanned conversations (and not just at scheduled learning times).
- Learning is emotionally engaging and memorable.
- Learning focuses on stories and pictures (rather than concepts and ideas).
- Learning relates to their own experience. (Consider inviting people to tell their stories. Then discuss how their experience relates to a Bible story or passage.)
- There is a mix of discussion and presentation.

Public Bible reading

'Until I come,' Paul tells Timothy, 'devote yourself to the public reading of Scripture, to preaching and to teaching' (1 Timothy 4:13). As we know, most people in the early church were illiterate and did not have direct access to the Bible. The only chance they had to encounter God's Word was through the public reading of Scripture. So the Word of God was heard rather than read. It was heard, recalled and retold.

Of course, today we have the Word of God, and most of us can read it. It would be crazy not to encourage people to read it for themselves. But we must not lose the public reading and hearing of God's Word. Jane Davis, founder of The Reader Organisation, has discovered that reading aloud is the best way to get people into books. She also recognized that it makes people 'calmer, happier, self-reflective, more sane and open-minded'! Her method has worked in retirement homes and with abused children, kids who have never read a thing, prisoners, residents on council estates and NHS patients.[8]

Steve Casey comments, 'Many of us are doing gospel work in areas of low literacy, but please don't take that as resistance to literacy. I have never met anyone in Speke who struggled with reading who didn't actually wish they could read better. The issue is how we make efforts to make a text more accessible to those who have often been scared off by it. Encourage people to hear the Bible being read out loud.'

From life to Bible to life

As we have seen, interactive Bible studies can feel like English comprehension exercises, especially when they are very text-focused. Yet a lot of evidence suggests that adults learn best when they are involved in their learning. So how do we run Bible studies for non-book people? The following model is adapted from an approach developed by Unlock (www.unlock.org.uk).

1. Encourage people to share their stories and experience
- Use cartoons, news stories, video clips, stories.
- Has something similar ever happened to you?
- What have our stories got in common?

2. Make links to the Bible
- Look for links with and differences from Bible stories.
- Ask 'what?' and 'why?'
- Focus on people rather than on texts. ('Why does Jesus say this?' rather than 'Why does verse 18 say this?')
- What can we learn from the Bible about our experiences?

3. Move towards change

- What difference will the links with the Bible make to us?
- Are there things we need to change?
- What would Jesus or Paul tell us to do?
- What are we going to do now?

Non-book people can be intimidated by bookish people. If you tell them that a contribution is wrong or they've missed the point, they probably won't contribute again. Instead, invite the group to respond, or continue with the discussion until the truth has been clarified in people's minds.

Bob Ekblad, Executive Director of Tierra Nueva and the People's Seminary, has been studying the Bible using this kind of method with prisoners and other marginalized people for many years. He writes,

> The interface between the reading and study of Scripture and contemporary reading of our contexts requires deliberate work and creativity. The following suggestions merely point the way . . . First choose whether you plan to begin with a chosen Scripture or begin with people's (or a particular) question or current struggle. If you plan to come to a group with a text or issue already chosen, begin at #2 below, before determining the question at #1.
>
> 1. Begin with a question that evokes the contemporary context and burning issue(s) of the people with whom you read. Sample questions include: 'What struggles, trials, temptations, challenges are you [or the other with whom you read] facing?' 'What are the external forces that are tempting, oppressing, or in any way obstacles to God's call on your or another's life?'
> 2. Look for a Scripture text that may speak into the life situation or sickness that you discern as the one that needs to be addressed.

How do you determine which text for which situation? Ask yourself: 'What is the heart of the matter in the text? What is the deeper meaning?' . . . [9]

Here is one example of this approach in action. Ekblad describes looking at Genesis 1:1–3 (NRSV) with a group of prisoners: 'In the beginning when God created the heavens and the earth, the earth was a formless void and darkness covered the face of the deep, while a wind from God swept over the face of the waters.'

'Here at the beginning, when God was creating the world, what were things like, according to this verse?' I ask a group of men.

People look down at their Bibles silently.

'It was chaotic. There was nothing,' someone ventures.

'There was darkness over the deep,' another man adds.

'Yes – this is talking about a place where everything is out of control, chaotic and dark,' I say. 'So do things ever seem that way now? Or has everything changed since then?' I probe.

'It's the same, man. Things are dark now too, really dark,' someone ventures. Others nod their agreement.

'So, do you feel the darkness? When and where do you notice this?' I ask.

'Right now in this place,' a man interjects.

'Outside too, things are bad. Chaos reigns. Drugs and s***, they're all over, man,' someone else adds.

The men talk about their struggles with feelings of isolation, loneliness, and fear . . .

It is easy for people on the streets or in the jail to talk about chaos, darkness, and the depths, and Genesis 1 suddenly seems like here and now.

'So what else do these first words of the Bible tell us about the beginning?' I ask, trying to move the study along in the direction of new hope.

'This says that "In the beginning when God created . . .",' a man slowly reads.

'OK,' I probe, 'so right there in the chaos and dark God was creating something too?'

We talk about how, according to Genesis, God is at work creating, right there in the heart of chaos and darkness.

'So, how is God creating?' I ask. 'What is God doing there in the darkness?'

'It says in my Bible the Spirit is hovering,' someone says. 'God is there, God is here,' he continues.

'Then God says: "Let there be light", and there was light,' another guy reads. 'God speaks to us, and that brings light.'

'So, what did the darkness have to do to experience the light? Did the chaos have to get its act together before God could come and speak?' I ask, trying to draw attention to the grace at the heart of this text. I find myself unable to resist pointing out narrative gaps that undermine the expected moralism.

The men look down at their Bibles.

'*Nada*, the darkness was just dark. God was there and spoke,' someone says, looking intrigued.

'So do you think this can happen now? How might God be present and speak and bring light now in our darkness?' I ask.

The men answer quickly and confidently.

'God speaks now through this,' a guy says, holding up his open Bible. 'God can speak to us through someone like you.'

'We come here to these studies. You help us understand. I feel peace when I leave,' says another man.

I invite the men to be on the lookout for God to be present with them when they are back in their cells. If this story is still true now, then maybe God's Spirit is hovering over us, and God is ready to speak and bring light into our lives.[10]

In case this appears a mysterious process, let me isolate the key questions that Ekblad asks:

- What were things like in this story?
- Do things ever seem that way now?
- What was God doing there in the darkness?
- What did the darkness have to do to experience the light?

It's the question: 'Do things ever seem that way now?' that enables people to connect the Bible with their own experience and thereby engage with its message.

Non-formal contexts for learning

Where was teaching done in the Old Testament? 'These commandments that I give you today are to be upon your hearts. Impress them on your children. Talk about them when you sit at home and when you walk along the road, when you lie down and when you get up' (Deuteronomy 6:6–7). Sitting at home, walking along the road, lying down at night – in all the ad hoc moments of life.

It was the same in the ministry of Jesus. He taught in response to events, questions, encounters, healings, conflicts, arguments, in the context of life. We have found, in our context, that most learning and training takes place not through programmed teaching or training courses, but in unplanned conversations: talking about life, talking about ministry, talking about problems.

This means the prerequisite for effective discipleship among the urban poor is a shared life. We need life-on-life discipleship, in which all of life is a context for learning and growth. We need a culture in which it is normal to talk about Jesus while washing up, or to rebuke one another as issues arise, or to reflect biblically on what we are doing.

Central to the life of any church must be the corporate preaching and teaching of God's Word. But we need to see Bible teaching and discipleship extending well beyond this.

Jane Casey, from Speke Baptist Church in Liverpool, describes how their church recognized the need for ministry among women. At first, they assumed this would mean meetings and programmes where the Word was taught and people applied it to their lives. But they soon recognized different cultural perceptions of reliability. For some, this involved turning up to meetings on time. But for the women of Speke, it was much more about emotional reliability – being there for people. Moreover, in Speke, unforgiveness was prevalent and indeed praised. So when women fell out, they could not be persuaded to come to a meeting to resolve the issue. The church, therefore, recognized the need for informal, reactive Word ministry to accompany the formal, proactive ministry of the Sunday gathering. 'We need ministry that starts with the Word and applies it to life,' comments Jane. 'But we also need ministry that starts with life and brings it to the Word.' This is true in any situation, but particularly needed on council estates. 'Women in Speke,' says Jane, 'are mainly reactive, living life without a plan, responding to events as they happen.' What will help someone struggling with bitterness is not a Bible study that she can't manage to attend, but a gospel friend standing with her. 'So we meet up one-to-one, sometimes on a regular basis, sometimes more ad hoc, but with an intention of talking about Jesus. We've found that women on the estate readily do this, often more naturally than we do.'

A hermeneutic of obedience
I had been reading the Bible with a group of non-literate learners. They would see meanings in the text that were valid, but to my mind tangential. I would steer them back to 'the big

idea' or 'the melody line'. But they would veer off again. At first, I was frustrated. Then I let it go. 'No Bible study is perfect,' I told myself. 'The Holy Spirit is at work.'

But more recently, I have realized that they may be operating with a more biblical hermeneutic: a hermeneutic of obedience.

They do not come to the text asking, 'What does Ephesians 3 mean?' That is my Bible-teacher, literate-learning question. They come asking, 'How does this speak to me?' And so they grab at whatever connects with their lives. I keep trying to prise their fingers off this so they can grasp my big idea. But they are tenacious. So I ask myself, 'Who has the better hermeneutic?' The fear of the Lord is the beginning of wisdom. Obedience and understanding are closely correlated in the Bible. So maybe they have!

It is worth considering the Bible's own hermeneutical categories.[11] We typically teach the importance of context, syntax, etymology and so on. These are important controls. But, as a hermeneutical approach, they are a bit like discussing a symphony by talking about minor sevenths and time signatures. Chords, keys and time signatures matter, if the orchestra is going to play the music correctly. The musicians cannot read from the score whatever they choose. This is not how the composer would have us engage with her composition. She wants us to wonder, delight, experience the music. And here we are entering the territory of the Bible's own hermeneutical categories: sing, gaze, meditate, wonder, taste. These are the ways in which the Bible encourages us to engage with God's Word.

Take listening as an example. In the Bible, 'listening' involves paying attention and acting on what we hear. It's a hermeneutical stance. We often take control of conversations by talking; listening is letting others take control. People sometimes say, 'You're not listening to me.' It shows how we can hear information without really paying attention. The Bible encourages us to listen to God's Word: to stop trying to control the learning process and pay attention to the voice of God.

In early Methodism, John and Charles Wesley recognized the importance of hymnody as a way of teaching the members of their largely working-class movement. In Deuteronomy 31:19, God tells Moses, 'Now write down for yourselves this song and teach it to the Israelites and make them sing it, so that it may be a witness for me against them.' Charles Wesley wrote hundreds of hymns. Truth was learned not in a classroom, but as worship.

Working-class people may not readily engage with the text of Scripture through the equivalent of English comprehension exercises. But they can be invited in other ways to taste the goodness of the Lord and gaze in wonder upon his works.

CONCLUSION

Working in a deprived area is not a good way to make a name for yourself. Your church is unlikely to look successful by our current standards of success. In fact, many leaders struggle with how 'unimpressive' their ministry looks. And ministry in deprived areas is typically slow and full of setbacks. Sometimes people who seemed to be prospective leaders fall away. 'People boomerang,' says Mez McConnell. 'They come to you, get cleaned up, go away, come back wrecked, and so on. You can invest in someone's life every day and then they walk away.' Julian Rebera from Moulsecoomb in Brighton says,

> Moulsecoomb always scores on the stats for teenage pregnancy, domestic-violence instances, unemployment, alcoholism, anti-social behaviour. Ours is the seventh attempt to plant on the estate since

the war. Since we started in 1996, we have attempted, but failed, to plant into two other areas. Our numbers have fluctuated, but have recently decreased down to about twenty-five consistent regular adults. I find myself wondering if it has all been worth it and what we've achieved. But I'm pretty sure the people we have here just would not fit into conventional churches.

You may be from a middle-class background. You will be crossing a deep cultural divide as you live among people on a council estate or in an ex-mining town. You will be culturally out of your comfort zone. If you were preparing for mission abroad, you would expect to go through a period of adaptation to the culture. In the same way, you may find integration into your new context a long and slow process. Steve Casey reckons it took five years (with his children attending the local school) just to *begin* to be assimilated into the culture in Speke, Liverpool. This can be an isolating and frustrating experience.

Money is always a challenge in church life, but particularly tricky if your congregation are not wage earners or are existing on low incomes. Supporting staff may require funding from outside the church. Or you may need to think creatively about how to resource your ministry.

Raising a family on a council estate presents challenges and questions. Dai Hankey says, 'I've got four kids under the age of five who are now living in a world very different from the one I grew up in – and they haven't even reached primary school yet! I confess there are times that I question whether it's appropriate or even loving to raise my kids in such a rough environment.'[1] One church leader commented that he has counted the cost of raising his daughters on an estate, and he accepts the possibility that one of his daughters may be pregnant before she is twenty. This is a high price to pay. Yet one mum urged us to remember that there are hundreds and thousands of 'local' mums facing this same fear every day.

We must avoid the perception that the children of Christian families are good, and the estate will be a bad influence on them. This attitude implies that other social contexts will not be a bad influence, or that working-class sins are more to be feared than middle-class sins. Children will not 'turn out bad' because they live on a council estate – they were born bad, with sinful, selfish hearts. Duncan Forbes writes, 'I believe that my children are sinners who can corrupt the estate, and so my emphasis is on teaching them God's way, rather than worrying that they will turn out bad – they are already bad!'

Such are some of the challenges of reaching the unreached. But there are many joys as well. Just before Pete and Sharon Jackson moved into Kendray, they found that all the radiators had been stolen from the vicarage, and a man had been set on fire outside the church building in a drugs-related incident. Sharon had not wanted to come to Kendray, but God's leading was unavoidable. Now she says, 'I wouldn't live anywhere else.'

There is great joy in being able to introduce broken and desperate people to a faithful Saviour. Having tried alcohol, drugs, sex, they are often left hungry for something that truly satisfies. Church planters testify to how humbling and exciting it is to be involved in the lives of those who come to Christ in this way.

John was an alcoholic who had not worked for many years before he was saved. Now he is always present at church events and always eager to help. As he studied the Bible with his church leader, God showed him that he was stealing, by falsely claiming benefits. He has started training for work and is also having counselling for his alcoholism. After a year, his daily consumption was vastly reduced, and, more recently, he has been completely 'dry' for a sustained period for the first time in a decade. This is not a prosperity gospel, with short cuts and false expectations. But doing life God's way is bringing wholeness. His pastor is grateful to have his own eyes opened again to God's generosity, and to discover afresh that salvation encompasses so much more than a pietistic faith.

Church leaders often feel as though they have discovered a new richness to the gospel, as they have ministered in council estates. I have heard people say they have seen grace in the lives of other believers in a way they had never encountered it before. Others talk about learning to move from a private mentality ('my home is my castle') to a community mentality, a move that has been hard, but which has also brought many joys.

Many church leaders love the fact that issues are in the open where they can be addressed and resolved. One leader pitied friends pastoring large middle-class churches, where the same difficulties exist, but often under the radar. Hidden problems are harder to address, and become more poisonous when left unchallenged.

Sustaining ministry in unreached areas

Andy Mason from the World's End estate in London turns to the parable of the sower (Mark 4:1–20) for the convictions that keep him in his ministry:

1. Don't forget that you're the soil

Jesus is the main sower, not me. He is the sower on my estate. Jesus is sowing through us, but the Word of God does not originate with us. Fruitful gospel ministry does not start with skills or buildings or strategies, but with gospel change in our own hearts. We are the soil. We need the gospel as much as anyone does. Those who know the gospel best can become like the path in the parable, with the gospel just bouncing off us. We can know our gospel outlines, but be hardened to its message.

2. *It's all about the kingdom*

This parable is a picture of what *Jesus* is doing for the world. Our ministry is about his kingdom, not my kingdom, God's glory, not my reputation. It's about Jesus' agenda, not my agenda. And his agenda is huge: Jesus is taking over the world. Our ministry is just one small part of that big plan. I don't know what God will do with my ministry. I don't know his timing. But I do what I do, knowing it is part of his plan.

In war, people have different roles. Some are generals; other are infantry. Some advance; others get their heads blown off. Some partake in strategic defeats. But every element matters. And every element matters to God and his strategy, even the apparent defeats. Sometimes we can think what happens in our church is defining for the lordship of Jesus. All the ups and downs shape my view of God's kingdom. But there is a bigger picture. Sometimes I joke about having a hundred-year plan!

3. *The gospel is powerful, even when you seem to fail*

A seed is a small, rather pathetic image of ministry. We might prefer it if it was a gun. It can seem that guns and knives carry more influence on our estates. But what happens if you bury a gun? It rots and rusts. Guns and knives do not have the power of life in them. A seed, in contrast, can be trampled and forgotten. But it has life in it. And so does the gospel. The gospel can be trampled and forgotten. But it also has the power of life in it. It is good to be realistic in ministry. But it is important, too, to be realistic about the authority that has been given to Jesus (Matthew 28:18).

You might object, 'I've been working away and seen no response', or 'People have fallen away.' There have been times when I thought the only thing on my CV will be: 'Failed church planter'. But there is help in Mark 4:11–12. Jesus tells the disciples,

> The secret of the kingdom of God has been given to you. But to those on the outside everything is said in parables so that,
>
> > 'they may be ever seeing but never perceiving,
> >   and ever hearing but never understanding;
> > otherwise they might turn and be forgiven!'

Part of the ministry of Jesus is to blind people. Jesus quotes Isaiah, who was told that people would not listen to him. He was promised failure. In the parable, three-quarters of the seed fails. It is a story with inbuilt failure. But opposition is part of the plan. It is not outside of God's sovereignty, for we are not just bringing salvation; we are also bringing judgment. As long as you preach the gospel, even your failure is success, in God's plan.

4. Our goal is heart change, not gathering numbers of people
What is church growth? According to the parable of the sower, it is not about numbers, but about the fruit of changed lives. Gathering people to hear the Word is important, but the size of our Sunday congregation can all too easily become the focus and measure of how we feel about ourselves. The goal is not numbers, but heart change. You can gather numbers quickly through exciting activities, but changing hearts is hard and slow.

This brings a very different focus to the ministry. We don't need to feel insecure about leading a small church. Jesus had a small 'church' who all ran away when the crunch came! It means we can be bold in challenging unbelief, because we're not worried about people not attending. We can be comfortable about a slow pace of change. It means we can, and will, rely on God. If we are prayerless, it may be we have forgotten that heart change is the aim, because, when we aim for heart change, we are forced to realize it is not under our control. It means we leave a legacy. A church in our area fell apart when the pastor left. The pastor had been caring, but had not taught the gospel or confronted sin. When he left, there was nothing. I want to leave behind a legacy of changed lives.

5. Expect to win

It may be that it is the Lord's plan for you to get your head blown off or to be in full retreat. But he will win the war. The gospel is still powerful in the midst of failure. The parable ends with growth. It may be that, in our lifetime, we don't see results, but these may come in a hundred years' time. This means I can take risks and endure setbacks, because the gospel is going to win. If you plant a seed and return the next day to see what has happened, the answer will be, nothing. But it *is* growing.

Making a name for Christ

So ministering in a deprived area is not a great way to make a name for yourself. We don't want such ministry to be the new cool, with a kind of macho trading of horror stories. But it is a great way to make a name for Christ, for your ministry will be a testimony to Christ, the power of God and the wisdom of God:

> Brothers, think of what you were when you were called. Not many of you were wise by human standards; not many were influential; not many were of noble birth. But God chose the foolish things of the world to shame the wise; God chose the weak things of the world to shame the strong. He chose the lowly things of this world and the despised things – and the things that are not – to nullify the things

that are, so that no-one may boast before him. It is because of him
that you are in Christ Jesus, who has become for us wisdom from
God – that is, our righteousness, holiness and redemption. Therefore,
as it is written: 'Let him who boasts boast in the Lord.'

(1 Corinthians 1:26–31)

God chose the uneducated, we might paraphrase, to shame
the graduates, the people from deprived areas to shame the
wealthy, the marginalized to shame the respectable, so that
no-one can boast, so that no-one
can say, 'God chose me because of
my wealth or education or influence.'
Christ Jesus is our wealth and
wisdom, our righteousness, holiness
and redemption. 'Let him who
boasts boast in the Lord.'

*God chose the
uneducated, we might
paraphrase, to shame
the graduates, the
people from deprived
areas to shame the
wealthy . . .*

'Blessed are the poor in spirit,'
said Jesus at the opening of the
Sermon on the Mount (Matthew
5:3). Blessed are the broken people,
we might say. Among the broken people, in the deprived areas,
in the midst of mess – here God is reigning in grace. Here
blessing is to be found.

NOTES

Introduction

1. Jacinta Ashworth and Ian Farthing, 'Churchgoing in the UK' (Tearfund, 2007), p. 12.

2. Robert Wearmouth, *Methodism and the Common People of the Eighteenth Century* (Epworth Press, 1945), p. 263.

3. David Bebbington, 'God Made Them High or Lowly', *Third Way* 10:4 (April 1987), pp. 10–14.

4. For more on this issue, see David Bebbington, 'God Made Them High or Lowly'; David W. Bebbington, *Evangelicalism in Modern Britain: A History from the 1730s to the 1980s* (Unwin Hyman, 1989); A. D. Gilbert, *Religion and Society in Industrial England* (Longman, 1976); Roy Joslin, *Urban Harvest* (Evangelical Press, 1982); David Smith, *Transforming the World? The Social Impact of British Evangelicalism* (Paternoster, 1998).

5. Bebbington, 'God Made Them High or Lowly', p. 12.

6. John Mark Hobbins, *The Class Question and the Unreached City* (London City Mission Policy Unit, 2010), p. 21.

7. Bebbington, *Evangelicalism in Modern Britain*, p. 111.

8. Roy Joslin, *Urban Harvest* (Evangelical Press, 1982).

9. For more on the relationship between evangelism and social involvement, see Tim Chester, *Good News to the Poor: Sharing the Gospel through Social Involvement* (IVP, 2004).

10. Tim Chester, *Good News to the Poor* (IVP, 2004).

11. Bob Ekblad, *Reading the Bible with the Damned* (WJK, 2005), p. xv.

1. Contextualization in working-class and deprived areas

1. Roy Joslin, *Urban Harvest* (Evangelical Press, 1982), pp. 4–5.

2. Ibid., p. 2.

3. David Cannadine, *Class in Britain* (Yale, 1998).

4. Cited in Cannadine, *Class in Britain*, pp. 20 and ix.

5. Alessandra Buonfino and Geoff Mulgan, *Porcupines in Winter: The Pleasures and Pains of Living Together in Modern Britain* (The Young Foundation, 2006), p. 48.

6. Polly Toynbee, 'You Can't Cut £18bn from the Poorest without Pain', *The Guardian*, Saturday 19 February 2011, p. 35.

7. Owen Jones, *Chavs: The Demonization of the Working Class* (Verso, 2011).

8. Paul Watt, 'Respectability, Roughness and "Race": Neighbourhood Place Images and the Making of Working-Class Social Distinctions in London', *International Journal of Urban and Regional Research*, 30:4 (December 2006), pp. 787, 789.

9. Ibid., p. 779.

10. Ibid., pp. 779–780.

11. *Porcupines in Winter*, p. 6.

12. See www.lausanne.org/en/documents/lausanne-covenant.html/.

13. Ruby K. Payne, *A Framework for Understanding Poverty* (Aha! Process, 2005), p. 113.

14. Joslin, *Urban Harvest*, pp. 3–4, 50–51.

2. The culture of working-class and deprived areas

1. Ruby K. Payne, *A Framework for Understanding Poverty* (Aha! Process, 2005), p. 22.

2. Duncan Forbes, 'Barriers and Bridges to the Gospel from My Own Personal Council Estate Perspective', paper for Reaching the Unreached Working Group, 2010.

3. Payne, *Framework for Understanding Poverty*, p. 23.

4. Steve Casey, 'Case Study: Speke', Reaching the Unreached Conference, London, May 2009.

5. Payne, *Framework for Understanding Poverty*, pp. 51–53.

6. Ibid., pp. 42–43.

7. Martyn Lloyd-Jones, *Joy Unspeakable* (Harold Shaw Publishers, 1985), p. 121.

8. A. D. Gilbert, *Religion and Society in Industrial England* (Longman, 1976), p. 151.

9. Cited in Roy Joslin, *Urban Harvest* (Evangelical Press, 1982), p. 154.

10. Joslin, *Urban Harvest*, pp. 26–27.

11. Cited in Lewis Drummond, *Spurgeon: Prince of Preachers* (Kregel, 1992), pp. 215–216.

12. Mark Driscoll, *The Radical Reformission: Reaching Out without Selling Out* (Zondervan, 2004), pp. 132–133.

13. Adapted from Tim Chester and Steve Timmis, *Everyday Church: Mission by Being Good Neighbours* (IVP, 2011).

14. Adapted from Dai Hankey, 'Walking the Streets with Your Eyes Open', 4 November 2010, Reaching the Unreached blog (www.reachingtheunreached.org.uk/cultural/walking-the-streets-with-your-eyes-open/).

15. Ibid.

3. Key gospel themes for working-class and deprived areas

1. See Tim Chester, *Awakening to a World of Need: The Recovery of Evangelical Social Action* (IVP, 1993).

2. Martyn Lloyd-Jones, *The Christian and the State in Revolutionary Times* (Westminster Conference, 1975), p. 103.

3. Wayne L. Gordon, *Real Hope in Chicago* (Zondervan, 1995), p. 170.

4. Paul Watt, 'Respectability, Roughness and "Race": Neighbourhood Place Images and the Making of Working-Class Social Distinctions in London', *International Journal of Urban and Regional Research*, 30:4 (December 2006), pp. 786–787.

5. Adapted from a talk given by Duncan Forbes at the second Reaching the Unreached conference in Barnsley in 2010, entitled 'Why We Need to Preach God's Sovereignty' (www.reachingtheunreached.org.uk/conferences/2010/).

4. Evangelism in working-class and deprived areas

1. Hendrik Kraemer, 'Continuity and Discontinuity', *The Authority of Faith* (International Missionary Council, 1939), pp. 1–21; Willem A. Visser 't Hooft, 'Accommodation: True or False', *South East Asia Journal of Theology* 8:3 (January 1967), pp. 5–18; Lesslie Newbigin, *A Word in Season: Perspectives on Christian World Missions* (Eerdmans, 1994).

2. This material draws on ch. 5 of Tim Chester and Steve Timmis, *Everyday Church: Mission by Being Good Neighbours* (IVP, 2011).

3. Paul David Tripp, *Instruments in the Redeemer's Hands* (P&R, 2002), p. 43.

4. Adapted from Duncan Forbes, 'Council Estate Evangelistic Conversations', 2011.

5. From Tim Chester, *You Can Change* (IVP/Crossway, 2008/2010), ch. 5.

5. Discipleship in working-class and deprived areas

1. Timothy J. Keller and J. Allen Thompson, *Redeemer Church Planting Manual* (Redeemer Church Planting Centre, 2002), pp. 35–36.

2. Adapted from Ruby K. Payne, *A Framework for Understanding Poverty* (Aha! Process, 2005), pp. 82–86.

3. Jim Hart, 'Local Church Leadership in Urban Communities', in Michael Eastman and Steve Latham (eds.), *Urban Church: A Practitioner's Resource Book* (SPCK, 2004), p. 19.

4. Roy Joslin, *Urban Harvest* (Evangelical Press, 1982), pp. 196–197.

5. Dai Hankey, 'Raising Leaders from Raw Material', 15 October 2010 (www.reachingtheunreached.org.uk/church/raising-leaders-from-raw-material/). See also Wayne L. Gordon, *Real Hope in Chicago* (Zondervan, 1995), pp. 115–123.

6. Teaching the Word in a non-book culture

1. John Finney, *Finding Faith Today: How Does It Happen?* (British and Foreign Bible Society, 1992), p. 74.

2. Gavin Reid, *The Gagging of God* (Hodder & Stoughton, 1969), p. 31.

3. Mark Snowden, 'Orality: The Next Wave of Mission Advance', *Mission Frontiers* (Jan–Feb 2004).

4. Alison Flood, from 'The Week in Books', *The Guardian*, 4 April 2009, Review, p. 5.

5. Based on research in Chris Key et al., *Booked Out: Learning to Communicate the Gospel in a Non-Book Culture* (CPAS, 1995), and Neville Black and Jim Hart, *Learning Without Books* (Unlock, 1985).

6. See Ruby K. Payne, *A Framework for Understanding Poverty* (Aha! Process, 2005), p. 30.

7. Ibid., p. 28.

8. 'The Joy of Reading Out Loud', *The Times*, Saturday 2 October 2010.

9. Bob Ekblad, *Reading the Bible with the Damned* (WJK, 2005), p. 6.

10. Ibid., pp. 12–14.

11. I am indebted for this insight to Marcus Honeysett of Living Leadership (www.livingleadership.org).

Conclusion

1. For more on raising children in deprived areas, see Dai
   Hankey, 'Raising Kids on the Frontline', 28 October 2010
   (www.reachingtheunreached.org.uk/struggles/raising-kids-on-
   the-frontline/).

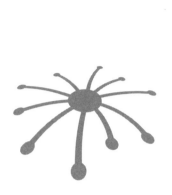

reaching
the
unreached

The Reaching the Unreached network exists to:

- provide a vforum for sharing and developing best practice between like-minded gospel workers in working-class and deprived areas;

- be an advocate for gospel work in working-class and deprived areas;

- develop resources for evangelism, discipleship and training in working-class and deprived areas.

The annual conference is held in late May each year.
Comments from previous delegates:

"Bible-centred, passionately delivered from those engaging in a real way"

"probably the most cutting edge and sorely needed conference in the entire calendar"

"I came expecting it to be really good, and found it to be even better"

For more information, and for audio and video resources from the conferences:

www.reachingtheunreached.org.uk